LIONEL MESSI

ARGENTINE FOOTBALLER

MR VIVEK KUMAR PANDEY

Contents

Foreword

Short Biography Of Lionel Messi About His Life Style,Career & Football History etc .During Writing This Book No Character, No Religion And No Caste Are Harmed. It's Only For Study Purpose.We don't want to hurt anyone. It's Only For Study Purpose.

Preface

Author biography in English :

MY NAME IS VIVEK KUMAR PANDEY . I WAS BORN IN 30 SEP 2002,I AM FROM SURAT GUJARAT INDIA.MY DREAM WAS TO BE GOOD WRITERS ,MY FAMILY SUPPORTED ME TO SUCCESSFUL AND I CAN DO IT MY SELF.How do I write? That is a question, I believe, that can be honestly answered by me."CELEBRATING YOUNGEST WRITER AWARD WINNER IN GUJARAT 1ST RANK" MR PANDEY JI . I may think I did a good job writing something. The reader is the one who decides the quality of my writing. I do find writing to be natural to me and therefore find it to be a real challenge. My trick as a challenged writer is to do the best I can and know that I am happy with the final outcome. It may take a while to do my best and there may be quite a few problems I run into along the way.

I am not a greedy person those who are thinking about me and my self I never tried it anyone people suffering from sadness ,I trying to get promoted people suffering from happiness and joy in your Life Time. Now in current situation in India and also world people are unemployed and have no many but our indian governor help to people to get free food from ration card , i also take part in leadership team ,i am Motivational speaker , Film script writer. There was my two dream firstly writer and secondly actor & also my own film is upcoming soon i done almost completely completed script for my film .I AM GOING TO SAY WORD OF HEART TOUCH OUT PLEASE READ IT" , firstly i thanks my father he supports me in this field they always getting inspired me by own his words and behavior ,they always said that he was a biggest person in the world in future and also they purchase fruit and chocolate for me in anytime & anyway , firstly my father buy him then call me Vivek you want a chocolate i will say yes papa but how many tell me ,papa: you tell me how much i buy him i told 1 or 2 chocolate but my father purchase whole the boxes of chocolate and they get suprised me. MY FATHER WAS BORN IN " 20 SEPTEMBER" 1971 IN INDIA.

1) MY FATHER FAVORITE CLOTHES IS KURTA PAIJMA AND ALSO STYLES SHOE

2) FAVORITE SINGER IS KISHORE DA

3) FAVORITE STATE GUJARAT AND KOLKATA , HIS VILLAGE IN BIHAR

4) FAVORITE COLOR BLACK AND WHITE

THEY ALSO LOVE cricket like IPL and one day t-20 .they also like watching a News daily and heard the song daily ,they also interested in tik tok video but in current time tik tok is banned in india but also few videos are in you tube. In lockdown time my family and me very enjoy day daily. my father play daily ludo with his sister and son, daughter.they always loved tea and coffee anytime call me . I make it tea for my father but some reason after the April to june they are suffering from fever and cough , weakness on 6 June 2020 my father death. they not told me say bye bye his life. After death of 6 June on 10 june my mom and dad anniversary.but my father is Best in the world they can do anything for me please take care of father and respect it of your parents.

ONE
LIONEL MESSI

- **Lionel Messi**

1. Short Biography Of Lionel Messi About His Life Style,Career & Football History etc .During Writing This Book No Character, No Religion And No Caste Are Harmed. It's Only For Study Purpose.We don't want to hurt anyone. It's Only For Study Purpose.

Lionel Messi, also known as Leo Messi, is an Argentine professional footballer who plays as a forward for Ligue 1 club Paris Saint-Germain and captains the Argentina national team. Widely regarded as one of the greatest players of all time, Messi has won a record seven Ballon d'Or awards, a record six European Golden Shoes, and in 2020 was named to the Ballon d'Or Dream Team. Until leaving the club in 2021, he had spent his entire professional career with Barcelona, where he won a club-record 35 trophies, including 10 La Liga titles, seven Copa del Rey titles and four UEFA Champions Leagues. With his country, he won the 2021 Copa América and the 2022 FIFA World Cup. A prolific goalscorer and creative playmaker, Messi holds the records for most goals in La Liga (474), most hat-tricks in La Liga (36) and the UEFA Champions League (8), and most assists in La Liga (192) and the Copa América (17). He has also the most international goals by a South American male (98). Messi has scored over 750 senior career goals for club and country, and has the most goals by a player for a single club (672).

Born and raised in central Argentina, Messi relocated to Spain at the age of 13 to join Barcelona, for whom he made his competitive debut aged 17 in October 2004. He established himself as an integral player for the club within the next three years, and in his first uninterrupted season in 2008–09 he helped Barcelona achieve the first treble in Spanish football; that year, aged 22, Messi won his first Ballon d'Or.

Three successful seasons followed, with Messi winning four consecutive Ballons d'Or, making him the first player to win the award four times. During the 2011–12 season, he set the La Liga and European records for most goals scored in a single season, while establishing himself as Barcelona's all-time top scorer. The following two seasons, Messi finished second for the Ballon d'Or behind Cristiano Ronaldo (his perceived career rival), before regaining his best form during the 2014–15 campaign, becoming the all-time top scorer in La Liga and leading Barcelona to a historic second treble, after which he was awarded a fifth Ballon d'Or in 2015. Messi assumed captaincy of Barcelona in 2018, and in 2019 he won a record sixth Ballon d'Or. Out of contract, he signed for Paris Saint-Germain in August 2021.

An Argentine international, Messi holds the national record for appearances and is also the country's all-time leading goalscorer. At youth level, he won the 2005 FIFA World Youth Championship, finishing the tournament with both the Golden Ball and Golden Shoe, and an Olympic gold medal at the 2008 Summer Olympics. His style of play as a diminutive, left-footed dribbler drew comparisons with his compatriot Diego Maradona, who described Messi as his successor.

After his senior debut in August 2005, Messi became the youngest Argentine to play and score in a FIFA World Cup in 2006, and reached the final of the 2007 Copa América, where he was named young player of the tournament. As the squad's captain from August 2011, he led Argentina to three consecutive finals: the 2014 FIFA World Cup, for which he won the Golden Ball, and the 2015 and 2016 Copa América, winning the Golden Ball in the 2015 edition. After announcing his international retirement in 2016, he reversed his decision and led his country to qualification for the 2018 FIFA World Cup, a third-place finish at the 2019 Copa América, and won the 2021 Copa América, while winning the Golden Ball and Golden Boot award for the latter. This achievement would see him receive a record seventh Ballon d'Or in 2021. In 2022, he captained his country to win the 2022 FIFA World Cup, for which he won the Golden Ball for a record second time, and broke the record for most appearances in World Cup tournaments with 26 matches played.

Messi has endorsed sportswear company Adidas since 2006. According to France Football, he was the world's highest-paid footballer for five years out of six between 2009 and 2014, and was ranked the world's highest-paid athlete by Forbes in 2019 and 2022. Messi was among Time's 100 most influential people in the world in 2011 and 2012. In February 2020, he was awarded the Laureus World Sportsman of the Year, thus becoming the first footballer and the first team sport athlete to win the award. Later that year, Messi became the second footballer and second team-sport athlete to surpass $1 billion in career earnings.

- **Lionel Messi life**

Messi was born on 24 June 1987 in Rosario, Santa Fe, the third of four children of Jorge Messi, a steel factory manager, and his wife Celia Cuccittini, who worked in a magnet manufacturing workshop. On his father's side, he is of Italian and Spanish descent, the great-grandson of immigrants from the north-central Adriatic Marche region of Italy, and on his mother's side, he has primarily Italian ancestry. Growing up in a tight-knit, football-loving family, "Leo" developed a passion for the sport from an early age, playing constantly with his older brothers, Rodrigo and Matías, and his cousins, Maximiliano and Emanuel Biancucchi, both of whom became professional footballers. At the age of four he joined local club Grandoli, where he was coached by his father, though his earliest influence as a player came from his maternal grandmother, Celia, who accompanied him to training and matches. He was greatly affected by her death, shortly before his eleventh birthday; since then, as a devout Roman Catholic, he has celebrated his goals by looking up and pointing to the sky in tribute to his grandmother.

"When you saw him you would think: this kid can't play ball. He's a dwarf, he's too fragile, too small. But immediately you'd realise that he was born different, that he was a phenomenon and that he was going to be something impressive."

Newell's Old Boys youth coach Adrián Coria shares his first impression of the 12-year-old Messi.A lifelong supporter of Newell's Old Boys, Messi joined the Rosario club when he was six years old. During the six years he played for Newell's, he scored almost 500 goals as a member of "The Machine of '87", the near-unbeatable youth side named for the year of their birth, and regularly entertained crowds by performing ball tricks during half-time of the first team's home games. However, his future as a professional player was threatened when, aged 10, he was diagnosed with a growth hormone deficiency. As his father's health insurance covered only two years of growth hormone treatment, which cost at least $1,000 per month, Newell's agreed to contribute, but later reneged on their promise. He was scouted by Buenos Aires club River Plate, whose playmaker, Pablo Aimar, he idolised, but they declined to pay for his treatment. His goalscoring idol growing up was Ronaldo, with Messi calling him "the best forward I've ever seen".

Messi enrolled at Barcelona's youth academy, La Masia, aged 13.

As the Messi family had relatives in Catalonia, they sought to arrange a trial with Barcelona in September 2000. First team director Charly Rexach immediately wanted to sign him, but the board of directors hesitated; at the time it was highly unusual for European clubs to sign foreign players of such a young age. On 14 December, an ultimatum was issued for Barcelona to prove their commitment, and Rexach, with no other paper at hand, offered a contract on a paper napkin. In February 2001, the family relocated to Barcelona, where they moved into an apartment near the club's stadium, Camp Nou. During his first year in Spain, Messi rarely played with the Infantiles due to a transfer conflict with Newell's; as a foreigner, he could only be fielded in friendlies and the Catalan league. Without football, he struggled to integrate into the team; already reserved by nature, he was so quiet that his teammates initially believed he was mute. At home, he suffered from homesickness after his mother moved back to Rosario with his brothers and little sister, María Sol, while he stayed in Barcelona with his father.

After a year at Barcelona's youth academy, La Masia, Messi was finally enrolled in the Royal Spanish Football Federation (RFEF) in February 2002. Now playing in all competitions, he befriended his teammates, among whom were Cesc Fàbregas and Gerard Piqué. After completing his growth hormone treatment aged 14, Messi became an integral part of the "Baby Dream Team", Barcelona's greatest-ever youth side. During his first full season (2002–03), he was top scorer with 36 goals in 30 games for the Cadetes A, who won an unprecedented treble of the league and both the Spanish and Catalan cups.

The Copa Catalunya final, a 4–1 victory over Espanyol, became known in club lore as the partido de la máscara, the final of the mask. A week after suffering a broken cheekbone during a league match, Messi was allowed to start the game on the condition that he wear a plastic protector; soon hindered by the mask, he took it off and scored two goals in 10 minutes before his substitution. At the close of the season, he received an offer to join Arsenal, his first from a foreign club, but while Fàbregas and Piqué soon left for England, he chose to remain in Barcelona.Barcelona's then assistant coach Henk ten Cate on Messi's first-team debut.

· **During the 2003–04 season**

his fourth with Barcelona, Messi rapidly progressed through the club's ranks, debuting for a record five youth teams in a single campaign. After being named player of the tournament in four international pre-season competitions with the Juveniles B, he played only one official match with the team before being promoted to the Juveniles A, where he scored 18 goals in 11 league games. Messi was then one of several youth players called up to strengthen a depleted first team during the international break. French winger Ludovic Giuly explained how Messi caught the eye in a training session with Frank Rijkaard's first team: "He destroyed us all... They were kicking him all over the place to avoid being ridiculed by this kid, he just got up and kept on playing. He would dribble past four players and score a goal. Even the team's starting centre-backs were nervous. He was an alien."

At 16 years, four months, and 23 days old, Messi made his first team debut when he came on in the 75th minute during a friendly against José Mourinho's Porto on 16 November 2003. His performance, creating two chances and a shot on goal, impressed the technical staff, and he subsequently began training daily with the club's reserve side, Barcelona B, as well as weekly with the first team. After his first training session with the senior squad, Barça's new star player, Ronaldinho, told his teammates that he believed the 16-year-old would become an even better player than himself. Ronaldinho soon befriended Messi, whom he called "little brother", which greatly eased his transition into the first team.

· **Messi playing against Málaga in 2005**

To gain further match experience, Messi joined Barcelona C in addition to the Juveniles A, playing his first game for the third team on 29 November. He helped save them from the relegation zone of the Tercera División, scoring five goals in ten games, including a hat-trick in eight minutes during a Copa del Rey match while man-marked by Sevilla's Sergio Ramos. His progress was reflected in his first professional contract, signed on 4 February 2004, which lasted until 2012 and contained an initial buyout clause of €30 million. A month later, on 6 March, he made his debut for Barcelona B in the Segunda División B, and his buyout clause automatically increased to €80 million. He played five games with the B team that season but did not score. Physically he was weaker than his opponents, who were often much older and taller, and in training he worked on increasing his muscle mass and overall strength in order to be able to shake off defenders. Towards the end of the season, he returned to both youth teams, helping the Juveniles B win the league. He finished the campaign having scored for four of his five teams with a total of 36 goals in all official competitions.

During the 2004–05 season, Messi was a guaranteed starter for the B team, playing 17 games throughout the campaign and scoring on six occasions. Since his debut the previous November, he had not been called up to the first team again, but in October 2004, the senior players asked manager Frank Rijkaard to promote him. Since Ronaldinho already played on the left wing, Rijkaard moved Messi from his usual position onto the right flank , allowing him to cut into the centre of the pitch and shoot with his dominant left foot. Messi made his league debut during the next match on 16 October, against Espanyol, coming on in the 82nd minute. At 17 years, three months, and 22 days old, he was at the time the youngest player to represent Barcelona in an official competition. As a substitute player, he played 244 minutes in nine matches for the first team that season, including his debut in the UEFA Champions League against Shakhtar Donetsk. He scored his first senior goal on 1 May 2005, against Albacete, from an assist by Ronaldinho, becoming – at that time – the youngest-ever scorer for the club. Barcelona, in their second season under Rijkaard, won the league for the first time in six years.

- **2005–2008: Becoming a starting eleven player**

"In my entire life I have never seen a player of such quality and personality at such a young age, particularly wearing the 'heavy' shirt of one of the world's great clubs." Fabio Capello praises the 18-year-old Messi following the Joan Gamper trophy in August 2005.

On 24 June, his 18th birthday, Messi signed his first contract as a senior team player. It made him a Barcelona player until 2010, two years less than his previous contract, but his buyout clause increased to €150 million. His breakthrough came two months later, on 24 August, during the Joan Gamper Trophy, Barcelona's pre-season competition. A starter for the first time, he gave a well-received performance against Fabio Capello's Juventus, receiving an ovation from the Camp Nou. While Capello requested to loan Messi, a bid to buy him came from Inter Milan, who were willing to pay his €150 million buyout clause and triple his wages. According to then-president Joan Laporta, it was the only time the club faced a real risk of losing Messi, but he ultimately decided to stay. On 16 September, his contract was updated for the second time in three months and extended to 2014.

· **Lionel Messi during a training session with Barcelona in 2006**

Due to issues regarding his legal status in the Royal Spanish Football Federation, Messi missed the start of La Liga, but on 26 September, he acquired Spanish citizenship and became eligible to play. Wearing the number 19 shirt, he gradually established himself as the first-choice right winger, forming an attacking trio with Ronaldinho and striker Samuel Eto'o. He was in the starting line-up in major matches like his first Clásico against rivals Real Madrid on 19 November, as well as Barcelona's away victory over Chelsea in the last 16 round of the Champions League,which came on back of an intense period of rivalry between the clubs leading a resentful Messi to state, "We would rather play Arsenal, Manchester United or anyone else than be on the pitch with Chelsea."After he had scored 8 goals in 25 games, including his first in the Champions League, in a 5–0 win over Panathinaikos on 2 November 2005, his season ended prematurely during the return leg against Chelsea on 7 March 2006, when he suffered a torn hamstring. Messi worked to regain fitness in time for the Champions League final, but on 17 May, the day of the final, he was eventually ruled out. He was so disappointed that he did not celebrate his team's victory over Arsenal in Paris, something he later came to regret.

While Barcelona began a gradual decline, the 19-year-old Messi established himself as one of the best players in the world during the 2006–07 campaign. Already an idol to the culés, the club's supporters, he scored 17 goals in 36 games across all competitions. However, he continued to be plagued by major injuries; a metatarsal fracture sustained on 12 November 2006 kept him out of action for three months. He recovered in time for the last 16 round of the Champions League against Liverpool, but was effectively marked out of the game; Barcelona, the reigning champions, were out of the competition. In the league, his goal contribution increased towards the end of the season; 11 of his 14 goals came from the last 13 games.

On 10 March 2007, he scored his first hat-trick in a Clásico, the first player to do so in 12 years, equalising after each goal by Real Madrid to end the match in a 3–3 draw in injury time. His growing importance to the club was reflected in a new contract, signed that month, which greatly increased his wages.

· Lionel Messi making his Maradona-esque run against Getafe in 2007

Already frequently compared to compatriot Diego Maradona, Messi proved their similarity when he nearly replicated Maradona's two most famous goals in the span of seven weeks. During a Copa del Rey semi-final against Getafe on 18 April, he scored a goal remarkably similar to Maradona's second goal in the quarter-finals of the 1986 FIFA World Cup, known as the Goal of the Century. Messi collected the ball on the right side near the halfway line, ran 60 metres (66 yd), and beat five defenders before scoring with an angled finish, just as Maradona had done. A league match against Espanyol on 9 June saw him score by launching himself at the ball and guiding it past the goalkeeper with his hand in similar fashion to Maradona's Hand of God goal in the same World Cup match. As Messi continued his individual rise, Barcelona faltered; the team failed to reach the Copa del Rey final after Messi was rested during the second leg against Getafe and lost the league to Real Madrid on head-to-head results.

After Ronaldinho lost form, Messi became Barça's new star player at only 20 years old, receiving the nickname "Messiah" from the Spanish media. His efforts in 2007 also earned him award recognition; journalists voted him the third-best player of the year for the 2007 Ballon d'Or, behind Kaká and runner-up Cristiano Ronaldo, while international managers and national team captains voted him second for the FIFA World Player of the Year award, again behind Kaká. Although he managed to score 16 goals during the 2007–08 campaign, the second half of his season was again marred by injuries after he suffered a torn hamstring on 15 December. He returned to score twice in their away victory against Celtic in the last 16 round of the Champions League, becoming the competition's top scorer at that point with six goals, but reinjured himself during the return leg on 4 March 2008. Rijkaard had fielded him despite warning from the medical staff, leading captain Carles Puyol to criticise the Spanish media for pressuring Messi to play every match. Barcelona finished the season without trophies, eliminated in the Champions League semi-finals by the eventual champions,

Manchester United, and placed third in the league.

- **Lionel Messi in 2008–09 First treble**

After two unsuccessful seasons, Barcelona were in need of an overhaul, leading to the departure of Rijkaard and Ronaldinho. Upon the latter's departure, Messi was given the number 10 shirt. He signed a new contract in July with an annual salary of €7.8 million, becoming the club's highest-paid player. Ahead of the new season, a major concern remained his frequent muscular injuries, which had left him side-lined for a total of eight months between 2006 and 2008. To combat the problem, the club implemented new training, nutrition, and lifestyle regimens, and assigned him a personal physiotherapist, who would travel with him during call-ups for the Argentina national team. As a result, Messi remained virtually injury-free during the next four years, allowing him to reach his full potential. Despite his injuries early in the year, his performances in 2008 saw him again voted runner-up for the Ballon d'Or and the FIFA World Player of the Year award, both times behind Cristiano Ronaldo.

Messi aiming to shoot during the 2009 UEFA Champions League Final against Manchester United.In his first uninterrupted campaign, the 2008–09 season, he scored 38 goals in 51 games, contributing alongside Eto'o and winger Thierry Henry to a total of 100 goals in all competitions, a record at the time for the club. During his first season under Barcelona's new manager, former captain Pep Guardiola, Messi played mainly on the right wing, like he had under Rijkaard, though this time as a false winger with the freedom to cut inside and roam the centre. During the Clásico on 2 May 2009, however, he played for the first time as a false nine, positioned as a centre-forward but dropping deep into midfield to link up with Xavi and Andrés Iniesta. He set up his side's first goal and scored twice to end the match in an emphatic 6–2 victory, the team's greatest-ever score at Real Madrid's Santiago Bernabéu Stadium.

Returning to the wing, he played his first final since breaking into the first team on 13 May, scoring once and assisting a second goal as Barcelona defeated Athletic Bilbao 4–1 to win the Copa del Rey. With 23 league goals from Messi that season, Barcelona became La Liga champions three days later and achieved its fifth double.

As the season's Champions League top scorer with nine goals, the youngest in the tournament's history, Messi scored two goals and assisted two more to ensure a 4–0 quarter-final victory over Bayern Munich. He returned as a false nine during the final on 27 May in Rome against Manchester United. Barcelona were crowned champions of Europe by winning the match 2–0, the second goal coming from a Messi header over goalkeeper Edwin van der Sar. Barcelona thus achieved the first treble in the history of Spanish football. This success was reflected in a new contract, signed on 18 September, which committed Messi to the club through 2016 with a new buyout clause of €250 million, while his salary increased to €12 million.

· **Lionel Messi in 2009–10 First Ballon d'Or**

His team's prosperity continued into the second half of 2009, as Barcelona became the first club to achieve the sextuple, winning six top-tier trophies in a single year. After victories in the Supercopa de España and UEFA Super Cup in August, Barcelona won the FIFA Club World Cup against Estudiantes de La Plata on 19 December, with Messi scoring the winning 2–1 goal with his chest. At 22 years old, Messi won the Ballon d'Or and the FIFA World Player of the Year award, both times by the biggest voting margin in each trophy's history.Arsène Wenger commends Messi for his four-goal display against Arsenal in April 2010.

The new year, however, started on a less positive note for Barcelona, as they were knocked out of the Copa del Rey by Sevilla in the Round of 16. Unsatisfied with his position on the right wing – with the club's summer acquisition Zlatan Ibrahimović occupying the central forward role – Messi resumed playing as a false nine in early 2010, beginning with a Champions League last 16-round match against VfB Stuttgart. After a first-leg draw, Barcelona won the second leg 4–0 with two goals and an assist from Messi. At that point, he effectively became the tactical focal point of Guardiola's team, and his goalscoring rate increased.

Messi scored a total of 47 goals in all competitions that season, equaling Ronaldo's club record from the 1996–97 campaign. He scored all of his side's four goals in the Champions League quarter-final against Arsenal on 6 April while becoming Barcelona's all-time top scorer in the competition. Although Barcelona were eliminated in the Champions League semi-finals by the eventual champions, Inter Milan, Messi finished the season as top scorer (with 8 goals) for the second consecutive year. As the league's top scorer with 34 goals (again tying Ronaldo's record), he helped Barcelona win a second consecutive La Liga trophy with only a single defeat and earned his first European Golden Shoe.

- **Lionel Messi 2010–2011 Fifth La Liga title and third Champions League**

Messi secured Barcelona's first trophy of the 2010–11 campaign, the Supercopa de España, by scoring a hat-trick in his side's second-leg 4–0 victory over Sevilla, after a first-leg defeat.Assuming a playmaking role, he was again instrumental in a Clásico on 29 November 2010, the first with José Mourinho in charge of Real Madrid, as Barcelona defeated their rivals 5–0. Messi helped the team achieve 16 consecutive league victories, a record in Spanish football, concluding with another hat-trick against Atlético Madrid on 5 February 2011. His club performances in 2010 earned him the inaugural FIFA Ballon d'Or, an amalgamation of the Ballon d'Or and the FIFA World Player of the Year award, though his win was met with some criticism due to his lack of success with Argentina at the 2010 FIFA World Cup. Under the award's old format, he would have placed just outside the top three, owing his win to the votes from the international coaches and captains.

Towards the end of the season, Barcelona played four Clásicos in the span of 18 days. A league match on 16 April ended in a draw after a penalty from Messi. After Barcelona lost the Copa del Rey final four days later, Messi scored both goals in his side's 2–0 win in the first leg of the Champions League semi-finals in Madrid, the second of which – a slaloming dribble past three Real players – was acclaimed as one of the best ever in the competition. Although he did not score, he was again important in the second-leg draw that sent Barcelona through to the Champions League final, where they faced Manchester United in a repeat of the final two years earlier.

As the competition's top scorer for the third consecutive year, with 12 goals, Messi gave a man-of-the-match performance at Wembley on 28 May, scoring the match-winning goal of Barça's 3–1 victory. Barcelona won a third consecutive La Liga title. In addition to his 31 goals, Messi was also the league's top assist provider with 18. He finished the season with 53 goals in all competitions, becoming Barcelona's all-time single-season top scorer and the first player in Spanish football to reach the 50-goal benchmark.

- **Lionel Messi and his teammates celebrating winning the 2011 FIFA Club World Cup**

As Messi developed into a combination of a number 8 (a creator), a 9 (scorer), and a 10 (assistant), he scored an unprecedented 73 goals and provided 29 assists in all club competitions during the 2011–12 season, producing a hat-trick or more on 10 occasions. He began the campaign by helping Barcelona win both the Spanish and European Super Cups; in the Supercopa de España, he scored three times to achieve a 5–4 aggregate victory over Real Madrid, overtaking Raúl as the competition's all-time top scorer with eight goals.

At the close of the year, on 18 December, he scored twice in the FIFA Club World Cup final, a 4–0 victory over Santos, earning the Golden Ball as the best player of the tournament, as he had done two years previously. For his efforts in 2011, he again received the FIFA Ballon d'Or, becoming only the fourth player in history to win the Ballon d'Or three times, after Johan Cruyff, Michel Platini, and Marco van Basten. Additionally, he won the inaugural UEFA Best Player in Europe Award, a revival of the old-style Ballon d'Or. By then, Messi was already widely considered one of the best footballers in history, alongside players like Diego Maradona and Pelé.

- **Lionel Messi in 2012 A record-breaking year**

"I feel sorry for those who want to compete for Messi's throne – it's impossible, this kid is unique."Pep Guardiola after Messi became Barcelona's all-time top scorer at the age of 24 in March 2012.As Messi maintained his goalscoring form into the second half of the season, the year 2012 saw him break several longstanding records. On 7 March, two weeks after scoring four goals in a league fixture against Valencia, he scored five times in a Champions League last 16-round match against Bayer Leverkusen, an unprecedented achievement in the history of the competition.

In addition to being the joint top assist provider with five assists, this feat made him top scorer with 14 goals, tying José Altafini's record from the 1962–63 season, as well as becoming only the second player after Gerd Müller to be top scorer in four campaigns. Two weeks later, on 20 March, Messi became the top goalscorer in Barcelona's history at 24 years old, overtaking the 57-year record of César Rodríguez's 232 goals with a hat-trick against Granada.Messi pointing to the sky following his record five-goal display against Bayer Leverkusen in the last 16 of the UEFA Champions League in 2012

Despite Messi's individual form, Barcelona's four-year cycle of success under Guardiola – one of the greatest eras in the club's history – drew to an end. Although Barcelona won the Copa del Rey against Athletic Bilbao on 25 May, its 14th title of that period, the team lost the league to Real Madrid and was eliminated in the Champions League semi-finals by the eventual champions, Chelsea, with Messi sending a crucial second-leg penalty kick against the crossbar.

In Barça's last home league match on 5 May, against Espanyol, Messi scored all four goals before approaching the bench to embrace Guardiola, who had announced his resignation as manager. He finished the season as league top scorer in Spain and Europe for a second time, with 50 goals, a La Liga record, while his 73 goals in all competitions surpassed Gerd Müller's 67 goals in the 1972–73 Bundesliga season, making him the single-season top scorer in the history of European club football.

Under manager Tito Vilanova, who had first coached him aged 14 at La Masia, Messi helped the club achieve its best-ever start to a La Liga season during the second half of 2012, amassing 55 points by the competition's midway point, a record in Spanish football. A double scored on 9 December against Real Betis saw Messi break two longstanding records: he surpassed César Rodríguez's record of 190 league goals, becoming Barcelona's all-time top scorer in La Liga, and Gerd Müller's record of most goals scored in a calendar year, overtaking his 85 goals scored in 1972 for Bayern Munich and West Germany.

Messi sent Müller a number 10 Barcelona shirt, signed "with respect and admiration", after breaking his 40-year record. At the close of the year, Messi had scored a record 91 goals in all competitions for Barcelona and Argentina. Although FIFA did not acknowledge the achievement, citing verifiability issues, he received the Guinness World Records title for most goals scored in a calendar year. As the odds-on favourite, Messi again won the FIFA Ballon d'Or, becoming the only player in history to win the Ballon d'Or four times.

· **Lionel Messi in 2013–2014 Messidependencia**

Barcelona had virtually secured their La Liga title by the start of 2013, eventually equalling Real Madrid's 100-point record of the previous season. However, their performances deteriorated in the second half of the 2012–13 campaign, concurrently with Vilanova's absence due to ill health. After losing successive Clásicos, including the Copa del Rey semi-finals, they were nearly eliminated in the first knockout round of the Champions League by AC Milan, but a revival of form in the second leg led to a 4–0 comeback, with two goals and an assist from Messi.

Now in his ninth senior season with Barcelona, Messi signed a new contract on 7 February, committing himself to the club through 2018, while his fixed wage rose to €13 million. He wore the captain's armband for the first time a month later, on 17 March, in a league match against Rayo Vallecano; by then, he had become the team's tactical focal point to a degree that was arguably rivalled only by former Barcelona players Josep Samitier, László Kubala and Johan Cruyff. Since his evolution into a false nine three years earlier, his input into the team's attack had increased; from 24% in their treble-winning campaign, his goal contribution rose to more than 40% that season."In Leo we are talking about the best player in the world and when things are not going well you have to use him. Even if he is half lame, his presence on the pitch is enough to lift us and our play in general."

After four largely injury-free seasons, the muscular injuries that had previously plagued Messi reoccurred. After he suffered a hamstring strain on 2 April, during the first quarter-final against Paris Saint-Germain, his appearances became sporadic. In the second leg against PSG, with an underperforming Barcelona down a goal, Messi came off the bench in the second half and within nine minutes helped create their game-tying goal, which allowed them to progress to the semi-finals. Still unfit, he proved ineffective during the first leg against Bayern Munich and was unable to play at all during the second, as Barcelona were defeated 7–0 on aggregate by the eventual champions. These matches gave credence to the notion of Messidependencia, Barcelona's perceived tactical and psychological dependence on their star player.

- **Lionel Messi during a game against Almería in 2014**

Messi continued to struggle with injury throughout 2013, eventually parting ways with his long-time personal physiotherapist. Further damage to his hamstring sustained on 12 May ended his goalscoring streak of 21 consecutive league games, a worldwide record; he had netted 33 goals during his run, including a four-goal display against Osasuna, while becoming the first player to score consecutively against all 19 opposition teams in La Liga. With 60 goals in all competitions, including 46 goals in La Liga, he finished the campaign as league top scorer in Spain and Europe for the second consecutive year, becoming the first player in history to win the European Golden Shoe three times. Following an irregular start to the new season under manager Gerardo Martino, formerly of his boyhood club Newell's Old Boys, Messi suffered his fifth injury of 2013 when he tore his hamstring on 10 November, leaving him sidelined for two months. Despite his injuries, he was voted runner-up for the FIFA Ballon d'Or, relinquishing the award after a four-year monopoly to Cristiano Ronaldo.

During the second half of the 2013–14 season, doubts persisted over Messi's form, leading to a perception among the culés that he was reserving himself for the 2014 FIFA World Cup. Statistically, his contribution of goals, shots, and passes had dropped significantly compared to previous seasons. He still managed to break two longstanding records in a span of seven days: a hat-trick on 16 March against Osasuna saw him overtake Paulino Alcántara's 369 goals to become Barcelona's top goalscorer in all competitions including friendlies, while another hat-trick against Real Madrid on 23 March made him the all-time top scorer in El Clásico, ahead of the 18 goals scored by former Real Madrid player Alfredo Di Stéfano. Messi finished the campaign with his worst output in five seasons, though he still managed to score 41 goals in all competitions.

For the first time in five years, Barcelona ended the season without a major trophy; they were defeated in the Copa del Rey final by Real Madrid and lost the league in the last game to Atlético Madrid, causing Messi to be booed by sections of fans at the Camp Nou. After prolonged speculation over his future with the club, Messi signed a new contract on 19 May 2014, only a year after his last contractual update; his salary increased to €20 million, or €36 million before taxes, the highest wage in the sport. It was reported that Vilanova played a key role in convincing Messi to stay amid strong interest from Mourinho's Chelsea.

- **Lionel Messi celebrating his second goal against Granada in 2014**

Under new manager and former captain Luis Enrique, Messi experienced a largely injury-free start to the 2014–15 season, allowing him to break three more longstanding records towards the end of the year. A hat-trick scored against Sevilla on 22 November made him the all-time top scorer in La Liga, as he surpassed the 59-year record of 251 league goals held by Telmo Zarra. A third hat-trick, scored against city rivals Espanyol on 7 December, allowed him to surpass César Rodríguez as the all-time top scorer in the Derbi barceloní with 12 goals. Messi again placed second in the FIFA Ballon d'Or behind Cristiano Ronaldo, largely owing to his second-place achievement with Argentina at the World Cup.

At the start of 2015, Barcelona were perceived to be headed for another disappointing end to the season, with renewed speculation in the media that Messi was leaving the club. A turning point came on 11 January during a 3–1 victory over Atlético Madrid, the first time Barça's attacking trident of Messi, Luis Suárez and Neymar, dubbed "MSN", each scored in a match, marking the beginning of a highly successful run.After five years of playing in the centre of the pitch, Messi had returned to his old position on the right wing late the previous year, by his own suggestion according to Suárez, their striker. From there, he regained his best form, while Suárez and Neymar ended the team's attacking dependency on their star player. With 58 goals from Messi, the trio scored a total of 122 goals in all competitions that season, a record in Spanish football.Messi dribbling past Juventus defender Patrice Evra during the 2015 UEFA Champions League Final

Towards the end of the campaign, Messi scored in a 1–0 away win over Atlético Madrid on 17 May, securing the La Liga title. Among his 43 league goals that season was a hat-trick scored in 11 minutes against Rayo Vallecano on 8 March, the fastest of his senior career; it was his 32nd hat-trick overall for Barcelona, allowing him to overtake Telmo Zarra with the most hat-tricks in Spanish football. As the season's top assist provider with 18 he surpassed Luís Figo with the most assists in La Liga. he made his record 106th assist in a fixture against Levante on 15 February, in which he also scored a hat-trick. Messi scored twice as Barcelona defeated Athletic Bilbao 3–1 in the Copa del Rey final on 30 May, achieving the sixth double in their history. His opening goal was hailed as one of the greatest in his career; he collected the ball near the halfway line and beat four opposing players, before feinting the goalkeeper to score in a tight space by the near post.

In the Champions League, Messi scored twice and set up another in their 3–0 semi-final victory over Bayern Munich, now under the stewardship of Guardiola. His second goal, which came only three minutes after his first, saw him chip the ball over goalkeeper Manuel Neuer after his dribble past Jérôme Boateng had made the defender drop to the ground; it went viral, becoming the year's most tweeted about sporting moment, and was named the best goal of the season by UEFA. Despite a second-leg loss, Barcelona progressed to the final on 6 June in Berlin, where they defeated Juventus 3–1 to win their second treble, becoming the first team in history to do so.

Although Messi did not score, he participated in each of his side's goals, particularly the second as he forced a parried save from goalkeeper Gianluigi Buffon from which Suárez scored the match-winning goal on the rebound. In addition to being the top assist provider with six assists, Messi finished the competition as the joint top scorer with ten goals, which earned him the distinction of being the first player ever to achieve the top scoring mark in five Champions League seasons. For his efforts during the season, he received the UEFA Best Player in Europe award for a second time.

- **Lionel Messi in 2015–16 Domestic success**

Messi opened the 2015–16 season by scoring twice from free kicks in Barcelona's 5–4 victory (after extra time) over Sevilla in the UEFA Super Cup. On 16 September, he became the youngest player to make 100 appearances in the UEFA Champions League in a 1–1 away draw to Roma. After a knee injury, he returned to the pitch on 21 November, making a substitute appearance in Barcelona's 4–0 away win over rivals Real Madrid in El Clásico. Messi capped off the year by winning the 2015 FIFA Club World Cup Final on 20 December, collecting his fifth club trophy of 2015 as Barcelona defeated River Plate 3–0 in Yokohama. On 30 December, Messi scored on his 500th appearance for Barcelona, in a 4–0 home win over Real Betis.

On 11 January 2016, Messi won the FIFA Ballon d'Or for a record fifth time in his career. On 3 February, he scored a hat-trick in Barcelona's 7–0 win against Valencia in the first leg of the Copa del Rey semi-final at the Camp Nou. In a 6–1 home win against Celta Vigo in the league, Messi assisted Suárez from a penalty kick. Some saw it as "a touch of genius", while others criticised it as being disrespectful to the opponent. The Celta players never complained and their coach defended the penalty, stating, "Barca's forwards are very respectful." The penalty routine has been compared to that of Barça icon Johan Cruyff in 1982, who was battling lung cancer, leading many fans to indicate that the penalty was a tribute to him. Cruyff himself was "very happy" with the play, insisting "it was legal and entertaining".

On 17 February, Messi reached his 300th league goal in a 1–3 away win against Sporting de Gijón. A few days later, he scored both goals in Barcelona's 0–2 win against Arsenal at the Emirates Stadium, in the first leg of the 2015–16 UEFA Champions League round of 16, with the second goal being Barcelona's $10,000^{th}$ in official competitions. On 17 April, Messi ended a five-match scoring drought with his 500th senior career goal for club and country in Barcelona's 2–1 home loss to Valencia. Messi finished the 2015–16 season by setting up both goals in Barcelona's 2–0 extra time win over Sevilla in the 2016 Copa del Rey Final, at the Vicente Calderón Stadium, on 22 May 2016, as the club celebrated winning the domestic double for the second consecutive season. In total, Messi scored 41 goals as Barcelona's attacking trio managed a Spanish record of 131 goals throughout the season, breaking the record they had set the previous season.

· **Lionel Messi in 2016–17 Fourth Golden Boot**

"[Messi] is indispensable, but the rest of us are dispensable. – No, the club is bigger than any manager, than any player... except Leo. That's the reality, and you have to accept it."In an interview with Barcelona's official magazine, Javier Mascherano outlines Messi's importance to the team.

Messi opened the 2016–17 season by lifting the 2016 Supercopa de España as Barcelona's captain in the absence of the injured Andrés Iniesta. he set-up Munir's goal in a 2–0 away win over Sevilla in the first leg on 14 August, and subsequently scored in a 3–0 win in the return leg on 17 August. Three days later, he scored two goals as Barcelona won 6–2 against Real Betis in the opening game of the 2016–17 La Liga season. On 13 September, Messi scored his first hat-trick of the season in the opening game of the 2016–17 UEFA Champions League campaign against Celtic in a 7–0 victory; this was also Messi's sixth hat-trick in the Champions League, the most by any player. A week later, Messi sustained a groin injury in a 1–1 draw against Atlético Madrid and was ruled out with injury for three weeks.

He marked his return with a goal, scoring three minutes after coming off the bench in a 4–0 home win over Deportivo de La Coruña, on 16 October. Three days after this, he netted his thirty-seventh club hat-trick as Barcelona defeated Manchester City 4–0. On 1 November, Messi scored his 54th Champions League group stage goal in Barcelona's 3–1 away loss to Manchester City, surpassing the previous record of 53 goals held by Raúl.

· **Messi finished the year with 51 goals**

Messi finished the year with 51 goals, making him Europe's top scorer, one ahead of Zlatan Ibrahimović. After placing second in the 2016 Ballon d'Or, on 9 January 2017 Messi also finished in second place – behind

Cristiano Ronaldo once again – in the 2016 Best FIFA Men's Player Award. On 11 January, Messi scored from a free-kick in Barcelona's 3–1 victory against Athletic Bilbao in the second leg of the round of 16 of the Copa del Rey, which enabled Barcelona to advance to the quarter-finals of the competition; with his 26th goal from a free-kick for Barcelona in all competitions, he equalled the club's all-time record, which had previously been set by Ronald Koeman. In his next league match, on 14 January, Messi scored in a 5–0 win against Las Palmas; with this goal, he equalled Raúl's record for the most teams scored against in La Liga (35).

On 4 February 2017, Messi scored his 27th free-kick for Barcelona in a 3–0 home win over Athletic Bilbao in the league, overtaking Koeman as the club's all-time top-scorer from free-kicks. On 23 April, Messi scored twice in a 3–2 away win over Real Madrid. His game-winning goal in stoppage time was his 500th for Barcelona. His memorable celebration saw him taking off his Barcelona shirt and holding it up to incensed Real Madrid fans – with his name and number facing the crowd. On 27 May, Messi scored a goal and set up another for Paco Alcácer in the 2017 Copa del Rey Final, helping Barcelona to a 3–1 victory over Alavés, and was named Man of the Match. In total, Messi finished the 2016–17 season with 54 goals, while his 37 goals in La Liga saw him claim both the Pichichi and European Golden Boot Awards for the fourth time in his career.

· **Lionel Messi in 2017–18 Domestic double and a record fifth Golden Boot**

Messi opened the 2017–18 season by converting a penalty in Barcelona's 1–3 first leg home defeat to Real Madrid in Supercopa de España. Thereby, Messi also extended his El Clásico goalscoring record with the goal being his 24th official and 25th overall. On 9 September, Messi scored his first hat-trick of the 2017–18 league campaign, against Espanyol in Derbi barceloní, thus helping to secure a 5–0 home victory for Blaugrana over local rivals. Messi netted twice against Gianluigi Buffon, on 12 September, as Barça defeated the last season's Italian champions Juventus 3–0 at home in the UEFA Champions League. On 19 September, Messi found the net four times in a 6–1 trashing of Eibar at the Camp Nou in La Liga. Three weeks later, on 1 October, Messi surpassed his former teammate Carles Puyol to become the third highest appearance maker in the club's history, as he helped Barça defeat Las Palmas 3–0 by assisting Sergio Busquets' opener and later adding two himself in his 594th official game for the club; the league game was played behind closed doors at the Camp Nou due to violence in Catalonia relating to an ongoing independence referendum.

On 18 October, in his 122nd European club appearance, Messi scored his 97th UEFA Champions League goal, and his 100th in all UEFA club competitions, in a 3–1 home victory over Olympiacos. Messi became only the second player after Cristiano Ronaldo to reach this century milestone, but accomplished it in 21 fewer appearances than the Portuguese counterpart. On 4 November, he made his 600th appearance for Barcelona in a 2–1 home win over Sevilla in La Liga. Following the reception of his fourth Golden Boot, Messi signed a new deal with Barcelona on 25 November, keeping him with the club through the 2020–21 season. His buyout clause was set at €700 million.

On 7 January 2018, Messi made his 400th La Liga appearance with Barcelona in a 3–0 home win over Levante, marking the occasion with his 144th league assist and 365th league goal for the club, the latter of which saw him equal Gerd Müller's record for the most league goals scored for the same club in one of Europe's top five divisions.A week later, he broke the record, scoring his 366th La Liga goal from a free kick in a 4–2 away win against Real Sociedad.

On 4 March, he scored his 600th senior career goal from a free kick in a 1–0 home win over Atlético Madrid, in La Liga. On 14 March, Messi scored his 99th and 100th Champions League goals in a 3–0 home win over Chelsea, becoming only the second player after Cristiano Ronaldo to reach this landmark, in fewer appearances, at a younger age and having taken fewer shots than his Portuguese counterpart. His opening goal, which came after only two minutes and eight seconds, was also the fastest of his career, as Barcelona advanced to the quarter-finals of the competition for the eleventh consecutive season. On 7 April, he scored a hat-trick in a 3–1 win over Leganés including his sixth goal scored from a free-kick for the season, matching the record set by former teammate Ronaldinho.

He once again finished the season as the top scorer in La Liga, with 34 goals, which also saw him win his fifth Golden Shoe award. On 21 April, Messi scored Barcelona's second goal – his 40th of the season – in a 5–0 win over Sevilla in the 2018 Copa del Rey Final, later also setting up Suárez's second goal; this was Barcelona's fourth consecutive title and their 30th overall. On 29 April, Messi scored a hat-trick in a 4–2 away win over Deportivo de La Coruña, which saw Barcelona claim their 25th league title. On 9 May, Messi scored as Barcelona defeated Villarreal 5–1 to set the longest unbeaten streak (43 games) in La Liga history.

- **Lionel Messi in 2018–19 Captain, 10th La Liga title, and a record sixth Golden Boot**

With the departure of former captain Andrés Iniesta in May 2018, Messi was named the team's new captain for the following season. On 12 August, he lifted his first title as Barcelona's captain, the Supercopa de España, following a 2–1 victory over Sevilla. On 19 August, Messi scored twice in helping Barcelona defeat Alavés 3–0 in their first La Liga match of the season, with his first goal, a free kick that he rolled under the jumping Alavés wall, making history in being Barcelona's 6000th goal in La Liga.

On 18 September, Messi scored a hat-trick in a 4–0 home win over PSV Eindhoven in Barcelona's opening Champions League group stage match of the season, setting a new record for most hat-tricks in the competition, with eight. On 20 October, Messi scored in a 4–2 home win over Sevilla, but was later forced off in the 26th minute after falling awkwardly and injuring his right arm; tests later confirmed that he had fractured his radial bone, ruling him out for approximately three weeks. On 8 December, Messi scored two free kicks – his ninth and tenth goals from set pieces during the calendar year – in a 4–0 away win over Derbi barceloní rivals Espanyol in La Liga; this was the first time ever that he had managed such a feat in the league. His first goal was also his 10th league goal of the season, making him the first player ever to reach double figures in La Liga for 13 consecutive seasons.

- **Lionel Messi taking a free-kick against Real Valladolid in 2018**

On 13 January 2019, Messi scored his 400th La Liga goal in his 435th league appearance in a 3–0 home win over Eibar, becoming the first player ever to manage this tally in just one of Europe's top five leagues. On 2 February, Messi scored twice in a 2–2 draw against Valencia, with his first goal coming from the penalty spot, his 50th La Liga penalty goal; as such, he became only the third player in La Liga history after Cristiano Ronaldo and Hugo Sánchez to score 50 penalties in the competition. Later that month, the club admitted they had begun preparations for Messi's future retirement.

On 23 February, Messi scored the 50th hat-trick of his career and also provided an assist for Suárez, as he helped Barcelona come from behind to achieve a 4–2 away victory over Sevilla in La Liga; the goal was also his 650th

career goal for club and country at senior level. On 16 April, Messi scored twice in a 3–0 home victory over Manchester United in the second leg of the Champions League quarter-finals to give Barcelona a 4–0 aggregate win, which saw Barcelona progress to the semi-finals of the competition for the first time since 2015; these were also his first goals in the Champions League quarter-finals since 2013.

On 27 April, Messi came off the bench and scored the only goal in a 1–0 home win over Levante, which allowed Barcelona to clinch the league title. this was his 450th La Liga appearance, and his first league title as Barcelona's captain. On 1 May, Messi scored twice in a 3–0 home win over Liverpool in the first leg of the Champions League semi-finals; his second goal of the match, a 35-yard free kick, was the 600th senior club goal of his career, all of which had been scored with Barcelona. In the return leg six days later at Anfield, Barcelona suffered a 4–0 away defeat, which saw Liverpool advance to the final 4–3 on aggregate. On 19 May, in Barcelona's final La Liga match of the season, Messi scored twice in a 2–2 away draw against Eibar (his 49th and 50th goals of the season in all competitions), which saw him capture his sixth Pichichi Trophy as the league's top scorer, with 36 goals in 34 appearances; with six titles, he equalled Zarra as the player with the most top-scorer awards in La Liga. He also captured his sixth Golden Shoe award, and a record third consecutive award since the 2016–17 season. On 25 May, Messi scored his final goal of the season in a 2–1 defeat to Valencia in the 2019 Copa del Rey Final.

- **Lionel Messi in 2019–20 A record sixth Ballon d'Or**

On 5 August 2019, it was announced that Messi would miss Barcelona's US tour after sustaining a right calf injury. On 19 August, Messi's chipped goal from the edge of the box against Real Betis was nominated for the 2019 FIFA Puskás Award. Later that month, he suffered another setback following the return of his calf injury, which ruled him out of the opening game of the season as a result, he was sidelined indefinitely, and was only expected to return to action with Barcelona after the September international break. On 2 September, Messi was shortlisted as one of the three finalists for both the 2019 FIFA Puskás Award and the 2019 Best FIFA Men's Player Award, with Messi winning the latter on 23 September.Messi's six Ballon d'Or awards on display in the FC Barcelona Museum. His record sixth from 2019 is at the front.

Messi made his first appearance of the season on 17 September, and on 6 October he scored his first goal of the season with a free kick in a 4–0 home win over Sevilla; this was his 420th goal in La Liga, which saw him break Cristiano Ronaldo's record of 419 goals scored in Europe's top five leagues.On 23 October, Messi scored his first Champions League goal of the season in a 2–1 away win over Slavia Prague, becoming the first player to score in 15 consecutive Champions League seasons (excluding qualifying rounds). He also equalled Raúl and Cristiano Ronaldo's shared record of the most sides scored against in the competition (33).

On 29 October, Messi scored in a 5–1 home win over Real Valladolid in La Liga; his first goal – a set piece from 35 yards – was the 50th free-kick of his career. His goals (608) also saw him overtake Cristiano Ronaldo's senior goal tally (606) at club level. On 9 November, Messi scored three goals (including two free kicks) in a 4–1 home win against Celta Vigo. This was his 34th hat-trick in La Liga, equalling Cristiano Ronaldo's Spanish top-flight record. On 27 November, in what was his 700th appearance for Barcelona, Messi scored one goal and assisted two more in a 3–1 home win over Borussia Dortmund in the UEFA Champions League. Dortmund were the 34th team he had scored against in the competition, breaking the previous record of 33 held by Cristiano Ronaldo and Raúl. On 2 December, Messi was awarded a record-breaking sixth Ballon d'Or. On 8 December, Messi scored his record-breaking 35th hat-trick in La Liga with three goals in Barcelona's 5–2 home win over Mallorca.

On 22 February 2020, Messi scored four goals in a 5–0 home win over Eibar in La Liga. On 14 June, he scored in a 4–0 away win against Mallorca, becoming the first player ever in La Liga to score 20 goals or more in 12 consecutive seasons. On 30 June, he scored a panenka in a 2–2 home draw against Atlético Madrid in La Liga, to reach his 700th goal in his senior career for Barcelona and Argentina. On 11 July, Messi provided his 20th assist of the league season for Arturo Vidal in a 1–0 away win over Real Valladolid, equalling Xavi's record of 20 assists in a single La Liga season from 2008 to 2009 with 22 goals, he also became only the second player ever, after Thierry Henry in the 2002–03 FA Premier League season with Arsenal (24 goals and 20 assists), to record at least 20 goals and 20 assists in a single league season in one of Europe's top-five leagues.

Following his brace in a 5–0 away win against Alavés in the final match of the season on 20 May, Messi finished the season as both the top scorer and top assist provider in La Liga, with 25 goals and 21 assists respectively, which saw him win his record seventh Pichichi trophy, overtaking Zarra; however, Barcelona missed out on the league title to Real Madrid. On 9 August, in the Champions League round of 16 second leg versus Napoli at the Camp Nou, Messi scored the second goal and earned a penalty which led to a third goal and led his side to a 3–1 home victory and qualified 4–2 on aggregate for the quarter-finals against Bayern Munich. On 15 August, Messi suffered his worst defeat as a player as Bayern Munich beat Barcelona 8–2 in a one-off tie in Lisbon, leading to another disappointing exit from the Champions League.

· **Lionel Messi in August 2020 Desire to leave Barcelona**

Following growing dissatisfaction with the direction of Barcelona on and off the field, Barcelona announced that Messi sent the club "a document expressing his desire to leave" on 25 August 2020. The announcement garnered a significant media response, including from current and former teammates and Catalan president Quim Torra. On 26 August, Barcelona's sporting director Ramon Planes iterated the club's desire to "build a team around the most important player in the world" and affirmed Messi will only be able to leave should a buyer pay his €700 million buyout clause; a reported early termination option available in Messi's contract could only be exercised if he had communicated his decision to Barcelona by 31 May 2020, although the player's representatives argued the deadline should be set to 31 August, due to the adjourned 2019–20 season. On 30 August, La Liga issued a statement stating Messi's contract and buyout clause were still active.

On 4 September, Jorge Messi, Lionel's father and agent, released a statement in response to La Liga claiming the release clause "is not valid when the termination of the contract is by the player's unilateral decision from the end of the 2019–20 season", as stated in Messi's contract with Barcelona moments later, La Liga issued a response reiterating their statement published on 30 August. Later that evening, Messi announced in an interview with Goal that he would continue at Barcelona for the final year of his contract. In the interview, Messi claimed to have informed Barcelona of his desire to leave multiple times, and club president Josep Maria Bartomeu said Messi could decide at the end of every season if he wanted to stay or leave, only for Bartomeu to refer to the release clause. This left Messi with two options: to stay or go to court against the club, with the player saying "I would never go to court against the club of my life".

- **Lionel Messi in 2020–21 Final season at Barcelona**

On 27 September, Messi began the 2020–21 season by scoring a penalty in a 4–0 home win against Villarreal in La Liga. Two days prior to the opening game, he again criticised the club, this time for the manner of Luis Suárez's departure, stating, "at this stage nothing surprises me any more". On 20 October, Messi scored a penalty in a 5–1 home victory against Ferencváros in the Champions League, becoming the first player in history to score in sixteen consecutive Champions League seasons. On 25 November, Messi was nominated for the 2020 Best FIFA Men's Player award, and was later shortlisted as one of the final three candidates.

On 29 November, Messi scored his side's fourth goal in their 4–0 victory over Osasuna. After scoring, he unveiled a shirt of his former side Newell's Old Boys, in tribute to Argentine compatriot Diego Maradona, who had died four days earlier, and raised both hands to the screen showing Maradona's face in the stadium. The shirt was a number 10 replica of the same one Maradona had worn during his stint with the club in 1993. On 17 December, Messi finished third in The Best FIFA Men's Player award behind Robert Lewandowski and Cristiano Ronaldo, and was included in the FIFA FIFPro World XI for the fourteenth consecutive year.

On 23 December, Messi scored his 644th goal for Barcelona against Real Valladolid in La Liga, surpassing Pelé with Santos as the player with the most goals scored for a single club. In order to celebrate his achievement, Budweiser sent personalised bottles of beer to every goalkeeper whom Messi has scored against. On 17 January 2021, Messi was sent off for the first time in his club career for violent conduct in the final minutes of Barcelona's 2–3 extra time defeat to Athletic Bilbao in the 2020–21 Supercopa de España Final. On 10 March, Messi scored from 35 yards out and later had a penalty saved in a 1–1 draw against Paris Saint-Germain at the Parc des Princes in the second leg of the Champions League round of 16 as Barcelona were eliminated at this stage for the first time in 14 years by an aggregate score of 2–5 after having lost 1–4 at home on 16 February, with Messi scoring Barcelona's only goal in that game.

On 15 March, Messi scored two goals in a 4–1 win against Huesca. With the first goal, he became the first player in football history to score at least 20 goals in 13 consecutive seasons in the top five European leagues. On 21

March, he surpassed Xavi's record to reach a club record of 768 appearances, in which he also scored a brace in a 6–1 away win against Real Sociedad. On 17 April, Messi scored twice as Barcelona defeated Athletic Bilbao 4–0 in the 2021 Copa del Rey Final. With his second goal, he broke Gerd Müller's record of 30 plus goals in 12 consecutive club seasons, setting a new record of 13. With his 35th trophy with Barcelona, Messi also overtook former Manchester United winger Ryan Giggs as the most decorated footballer for a single club. On 16 May, Messi scored his 30th league goal of the campaign in a 1–2 home defeat against Celta Vigo, which later turned out to be his final goal and match in a Barcelona shirt.

The top goalscorer in La Liga, Messi was announced as the winner of the Pichichi trophy for a record eighth time in his career. It was also his record fifth consecutive win in La Liga, surpassing Alfredo Di Stéfano and Hugo Sánchez who both had four for Real Madrid, and equalled former Marseille striker Jean-Pierre Papin's record of five consecutive league top scorer awards in the top five leagues of Europe.

"Leo wanted to stay and the Club wanted him to stay but with the La Liga rules it has not been possible. To comply with the league's fair play regulations we had to accept an agreement that mortgaged the Club's TV right for half a century and FC Barcelona is above everything else."

On 1 July, Messi became a free agent after his contract expired, with negotiations on a new deal complicated due to financial issues at Barcelona. On 5 August, Barcelona announced that Messi would not be staying at the club, even though both parties reached an agreement and were due to sign a contract that day. The club cited financial and structural obstacles posed by La Liga regulations as a reason for Messi's departure. Club president Joan Laporta also blamed the previous board for Messi's exit by saying "the basis of everything is the calamitous and disastrous situation left by the previous board", he added by saying "the expected debt is much higher and we had some sports contracts in place that meant we had no margin on salary". Three days later, in a tearful press conference held at the Camp Nou, Messi confirmed that he would be leaving Barcelona.

On 10 August, Messi joined French club Paris Saint-Germain.He signed a two-year deal until June 2023 with an option for an extra year. Messi chose 30 as his squad number, the same he wore as a teenager when he made his senior debut for Barcelona.

Messi made his debut for the club on 29 August, coming on as a substitute in the second half of a 2–0 away win over Reims in Ligue 1. He made his first start and Champions League debut for the club in a 1–1 away draw against Club Brugge on 15 September. Four days later, Messi made his home debut for PSG in a 2–1 win over Lyon. On 28 September, he scored his first goal for the club, a strike from the edge of the 18-yard box in a 2–0 Champions League group stage win over Pep Guardiola's Manchester City. On 21 November, Messi scored his first Ligue 1 goal in a 3–1 home victory over Nantes. Later that month, he provided a hat-trick of assists for the fifth time in his career as PSG beat Saint-Étienne 3–1 away from home. Having scored 40 goals at club and international level for the calendar year and helped Argentina win the 2021 Copa América, Messi received a record seventh Ballon d'Or on 29 November.

"I think about being able to reverse the situation, about not having the feeling of having changed clubs and that it didn't go well for me. I'm already prepared for what's to come, I know the club, I know the city, I'm a little more comfortable with the dressing room, with my teammates and I know it's going to be different."

—

On 2 January 2022, PSG announced that Messi had tested positive for COVID-19, missing two league games and a cup game as a result. He made his return against on 23 January in the league against Reims where he came on as a substitute in the second half and assisted PSG's third goal in a 4–0 home victory. On 13 March, following their Champions League elimination against Real Madrid in the round of 16, Messi and his team-mate Neymar were booed by some of the PSG fans at the Parc des Princes in the league match against Bordeaux. Then-PSG manager Mauricio Pochettino defended Messi by saying "To judge Messi in this way is unfair," adding "It was a year of learning, and not just on a professional level coming to Paris Saint-Germain, in a new league and with new teammates, but also on a family level." On 23 April, he helped PSG clinch their 10th Ligue 1 title after scoring from a strike outside the 18-yard box in a 1–1 draw against Lens at home. Messi finished his debut season with 11 goals and 14 assists across all competitions. He failed to reach double figure league goals for the first time since 2005–06, ending the campaign with 6.

• Lionel Messi in 2022–23 Regained form

After adjusting to his new surroundings and settling in Paris, under new coach Christophe Galtier, Messi returned to his preferred free attacking role;

being placed in his favoured position as the playmaker behind two strikers, in a attacking trident with Neymar and Kylian Mbappé, quickly regaining his form from his previous season by starting off the new season on 31 July by scoring PSG's first goal in a 4–0 victory over Nantes in the Trophée des Champions, winning his second trophy with PSG.

Due to his previous form last season, Messi was not nominated for the Ballon d'Or award for the first time since 2005. On 21 August, Messi provided a long-range assist for Mbappé, clocked at eight seconds, for Ligue 1's second-fastest goal ever scored, before also scoring a goal in 7–1 away win over Lille. The following matches, after registering six goal contributions, including one goal and five assists, Messi was named Ligue 1's Player of the Month in September.

On 5 October, he scored in a 1–1 draw away to Benfica in the Champions League, becoming the only player in the competition's history to score against 40 different Champions League opponents. On 25 October, he scored twice in a 7–2 Champions League win at home to Maccabi Haifa, setting the record for the most goals scored from outside the 18-yard box than any other player in the competition, with 23 goals. Four days later, Messi scored and provided an assist as PSG won 4–3 against Troyes to remain top of the Ligue 1 table. The goal was his seventh of the league season and his twelveth overall, surpassing his total output of eleven goals in all competitions during the 2021–22 season in just 18 matches.

- **International career 2004–2005 Success at youth level**

As a dual Argentine-Spanish national, Messi was eligible to play for the national team of both countries. Selectors for Spain's Under-17 squad began pursuing him in 2003 after Barcelona's director of football, Carles Rexach, alerted the Royal Spanish Football Federation to their young player. Messi declined the offer, having aspired to represent La Albiceleste since childhood. To further prevent Spain from taking him, the Argentine Football Association organised two under-20 friendlies in June 2004, against Paraguay and Uruguay, with the purpose of finalising his status as an Argentina player in FIFA.

Five days after his 17th birthday, on 29 June, he made his debut for his country against Paraguay, scoring once and providing two assists in their 8–0 victory. He was subsequently included in the squad for the South American Youth Championship, held in Colombia in February 2005. As he lacked the stamina of his teammates, the result of his former growth hormone deficiency, he was used as a substitute in six of the nine games. After being named man of the match against Venezuela, he scored the winning 2–1 goal in the crucial last match against Brazil, thereby securing their third-place qualification for the FIFA World Youth Championship.

Aware of his physical limitations, Messi employed a personal trainer to increase his muscle mass, returning to the squad in an improved condition in time for the World Youth Championship, hosted by the Netherlands in June. After he was left out of the starting line-up in their first match against the United States, a 1–0 defeat, the squad's senior players asked manager Francisco Ferraro to let Messi start, as they considered him their best player.

After helping the team defeat Egypt and Germany to progress past the group stage, Messi proved decisive in the knockout phase as he scored their equaliser against Colombia, provided a goal and an assist against title favourites Spain, and scored their opening goal against reigning champions Brazil. Ahead of the final, he was awarded the Golden Ball as the best player of the tournament. He scored two penalties in their 2–1 victory over Nigeria, clinching Argentina's fifth championship and finishing the tournament as top scorer with 6 goals. His performances drew comparisons with compatriot Diego Maradona, who had led Argentina to the title in 1979.

- **Lionel Messi in 2005–2006 Senior and World Cup debuts**

In recognition of his achievements with the under-20 side, senior manager José Pékerman gave Messi his first call-up for a friendly against Hungary on 17 August 2005. Aged 18, Messi made his senior debut for Argentina in the Ferenc Puskás Stadium when he came on in the 63rd minute, only to be sent off after two minutes for a perceived foul against Vilmos Vanczák, who had grabbed his shirt; Messi had struck the defender with his arm while trying to shake him off, which the referee interpreted as an intentional elbowing, a contentious decision.

Messi was reportedly found weeping in the dressing room after his sending-off. He returned to the team on 3 September in their World Cup qualifier defeat to Paraguay, which he had declared his "re-debut" ahead of the match. Messi started his first game in the next qualifying match against Peru, in which he was able to win a crucial penalty that secured their victory. After the match, Pékerman described him as "a jewel". He subsequently made regular appearances for the team ahead of Argentina's participation in the 2006 FIFA World Cup, scoring his first goal in a friendly against Croatia on 1 March 2006. A hamstring injury sustained a week later jeopardised his presence in the World Cup, but he was nevertheless selected for Pékerman's squad and regained fitness in time for the start of the tournament.

During the World Cup in Germany, Messi witnessed their opening match victory against the Ivory Coast from the substitutes' bench. In the next match, against Serbia and Montenegro, he became the youngest player to represent Argentina at a FIFA World Cup when he came on as a substitute in the 74th minute. He assisted their fourth strike within minutes and scored the final goal in their 6–0 victory, making him the youngest scorer in the tournament and the sixth-youngest goalscorer in the history of the World Cup.

As their progression to the knockout phase was secured, several starters were rested during the last group match. Messi consequently started the game against the Netherlands, a 0–0 draw, as they won their group on goal differential. In the round of 16 match against Mexico, played on his 19th birthday, Messi came on in the 84th minute, with the score tied at 1–1. He appeared to score a goal, but it was contentiously ruled offside, with the team needing a late goal in extra time to proceed. He did not play in the quarter-final against Germany, during which Argentina were eliminated 4–2 in a penalty shootout. Back home, Pékerman's decision to leave him on the bench against Germany led to widespread criticism from those who believed Messi could have changed the outcome of the match in Argentina's favour.

As Messi evolved into one of the best players in the world, he secured a place in Alfio Basile's starting line-up, as part of a team considered favourites to win the 2007 Copa América, held in Venezuela. He set up the game-winning goal of their 4–1 victory over the United States in the opening match, before winning a penalty that led to the game-tying first strike of their 4–2 win in the next match against Colombia. At the quarter-final stage, where the group winners faced Peru, he scored the second goal of a 4–0 victory that saw them through to the semi-final, during which he chipped the ball over Mexico's goalkeeper to ensure another 3–0 win. In a surprise defeat, Argentina lost the final 3–0 to a Brazil squad that lacked several of the nation's best players. Their unexpected loss was followed by much criticism in Argentina, though Messi was mostly exempt due to his young age and secondary status to star player Juan Román Riquelme. He was named the best young player of the tournament by CONMEBOL.

Ahead of the 2008 Summer Olympics, Barcelona legally barred Messi from representing Argentina at the tournament as it coincided with their Champions League qualifying matches. After interference from newly appointed Barcelona manager Pep Guardiola, who had won the tournament in 1992, Messi was permitted to join Sergio Batista's under-23 squad in Beijing.

During the first match, he scored the opening goal in their 2–1 victory over the Ivory Coast. Following a 1–0 win in the next group match against Australia, ensuring their quarter-final qualification, Messi was rested during the game against Serbia, while his side won the match to finish first in their group. Against the Netherlands, he again scored the first goal and assisted a second strike to help his team to a 2–1 win in extra time. After a 3–0 semi-final victory over Brazil, Messi assisted the only goal in the final as Argentina defeated Nigeria to claim Olympic gold medals. Along with Riquelme, Messi was singled out by FIFA as the stand-out player from the tournament's best team.

· Lionel Messi in 2008–2011 Collective decline

From late 2008, the national team experienced a three-year period marked by poor performances. Under manager Diego Maradona, who had led Argentina to World Cup victory as a player, the team struggled to qualify for the 2010 World Cup, securing their place in the tournament only after defeating Uruguay 1–0 in their last qualifying match. Maradona was criticised for his strategic decisions, which included playing Messi out of his usual position. In eight qualifying matches under Maradona's stewardship, Messi scored only one goal, netting the opening goal in the first such match, a 4–0 victory over Venezuela.

During that game, played on 28 March 2009, he wore Argentina's number 10 shirt for the first time, following the international retirement of Riquelme. Overall, Messi scored four goals in 18 appearances during the qualifying process. Ahead of the tournament, Maradona visited Messi in Barcelona to request his tactical input; Messi then outlined a 4–3–1–2 formation with himself playing behind the two strikers, a playmaking position known as the enganche in Argentine football, which had been his preferred position since childhood.

· World Cup in South Africa

Despite their poor qualifying campaign, Argentina were considered title contenders at the World Cup in South Africa. At the start of the tournament, the new formation proved effective; Messi managed at least four attempts on goal during their opening match but was repeatedly denied by Nigeria's goalkeeper, resulting in a 1–0 win. During the next match, against South Korea, he excelled in his playmaking role, participating in all four goals of his side's 4–1 victory. As their place in the knockout phase was guaranteed, most of the starters were rested during the last group match, but Messi reportedly refused to be benched. He wore the captain's armband for the first time in their 2–0 win against Greece; as the focal point of their play, he helped create their second goal to see Argentina finish as group winners.

Argentina were eliminated in the quarter-final against Germany, at the same stage of the tournament and by the same opponent as four years earlier. Their 4–0 loss was their worst margin of defeat at a World Cup since 1974. FIFA subsequently identified Messi as one of the tournament's 10 best players, citing his "outstanding" pace and creativity and "spectacular and efficient" dribbling, shooting and passing. Back home, however, Messi was the subject of harsher judgement. As the perceived best player in the world, he had been expected to lead an average team to the title, as Maradona arguably did in 1986, but he had failed to replicate his performances at Barcelona with the national team, leading to the accusation that he cared less about his country than his club.

Maradona was replaced by Sergio Batista, who had orchestrated Argentina's Olympic victory. Batista publicly stated that he intended to build the team around Messi, employing him as a false nine within a 4–3–3 system, as used to much success by Barcelona. Although Messi scored a record 53 goals during the 2010–11 club season, he had not scored for Argentina in an official match since March 2009. Despite the tactical change, his goal drought continued during the 2011 Copa América, hosted by Argentina. Their first two matches, against Bolivia and Colombia, ended in draws. Media and fans noted that he did not combine well with striker Carlos Tevez, who enjoyed greater popularity among the Argentine public; Messi was consequently booed by his own team's supporters for the first time in his career. During the crucial next match, with Tevez on the bench, he gave a well-received performance, assisting two goals in their 3–0 victory over Costa Rica. After the quarter-final against Uruguay ended in a 1–1 draw following extra time, with Messi having assisted their equaliser, Argentina were eliminated 4–5 in the penalty shootout by the eventual champions.

• **World Cup in South Africa in 2011–2013 Assuming the captaincy**

After Argentina's unsuccessful performance in the Copa América, Batista was replaced by Alejandro Sabella. Upon his appointment in August 2011, Sabella awarded the 24-year-old Messi the captaincy of the squad, in accord with then-captain Javier Mascherano. Reserved by nature, Messi went on to lead his squad by example as their best player, while Mascherano continued to fulfil the role of the team's on-field leader and motivator. In a further redesign of the team, Sabella dismissed Tevez and brought in players with whom Messi had won the World Youth Championship and Olympic Games. Now playing in a free role in an improving team, Messi ended his goal drought by scoring during their first World Cup qualifying match against Chile on 7 October, his first official goal for Argentina in two-and-a-half years.

Under Sabella, Messi's goalscoring rate drastically increased; where he had scored only 17 goals in 61 matches under his previous managers, he scored 25 times in 32 appearances during the following three years. He netted a total of 12 goals in 9 games for Argentina in 2012, equalling the record held by Gabriel Batistuta for the most goals scored in a calendar year for their country.

His first international hat-trick came in a friendly against Switzerland on 29 February 2012, followed by two more hat-tricks over the next year-and-a-half in friendlies against Brazil and Guatemala. Messi then helped the team secure their place in the 2014 World Cup with a 5–2 victory over Paraguay on 10 September 2013 when he scored twice from penalty kicks, taking his international tally to 37 goals to become Argentina's second-highest goalscorer behind Batistuta. Overall, he had scored a total of 10 goals in 14 matches during the qualifying campaign. Concurrently with his bettered performances, his relationship with his compatriots improved, as he gradually began to be perceived more favourably in Argentina.

• **World Cup in South Africa in 2014–2015 World Cup and Copa América finals**

Messi watches his 25-yard curling strike hit the net against Iran to win the game for Argentina in their second group game at the 2014 FIFA World Cup.Ahead of the World Cup in Brazil, doubts persisted over Messi's form, as he finished an unsuccessful and injury-plagued season with Barcelona.

At the start of the tournament, however, he gave strong performances, being elected man of the match in their first four matches. In his first World Cup match as captain, he led them to a 2–1 victory over Bosnia and Herzegovina; he helped create Sead Kolašinac's own goal and scored their second strike after a dribble past three players, his first World Cup goal since his debut in the tournament eight years earlier.During the second match against Iran, he scored an injury-time goal from 25 yards out to end the game in a 1–0 win, securing their qualification for the knockout phase.

He scored twice in the last group match, a 3–2 victory over Nigeria, his second goal coming from a free kick, as they finished first in their group. Messi assisted a late goal in extra time to ensure a 1–0 win against Switzerland in the round of 16, and played in the 1–0 quarter-final win against Belgium as Argentina progressed to the semi-final of the World Cup for the first time since 1990. Following a 0–0 draw in extra time, they eliminated the Netherlands 4–2 in a penalty shootout to reach the final, with Messi scoring his team's first penalty.

- **Messi battles Germany's Mats Hummels for the ball during the 2014 FIFA World Cup final**

Billed as Messi versus Germany, the world's best player against the best team, the final was a repeat of the 1990 final featuring Diego Maradona. Within the first half-hour, Messi had started the play that led to a goal, but it was ruled offside. He missed several opportunities to open the scoring throughout the match, in particular at the start of the second half when his breakaway effort went wide of the far post. Substitute Mario Götze finally scored in the 113th minute, followed in the last minute of extra time by a free kick that Messi sent over the net, as Germany won the match 1–0 to claim the World Cup.

At the conclusion of the final, Messi was awarded the Golden Ball as the best player of the tournament. In addition to being the joint third-highest goalscorer, with four goals and an assist, he created the most chances, completed the most dribbling runs, made the most deliveries into the penalty area and produced the most throughballs in the competition. However, his selection drew criticism due to his lack of goals in the knockout round; FIFA President Sepp Blatter expressed his surprise, while Maradona suggested that Messi had undeservedly been chosen for marketing purposes.

Another final appearance, the third of Messi's senior international career, followed in the 2015 Copa América, held in Chile. Under the stewardship of former Barcelona manager Gerardo Martino, Argentina entered the tournament as title contenders due to their second-place achievement at the World Cup. During the opening match against Paraguay, they were ahead two goals by half-time but lost their lead to end the match in a 2–2 draw; Messi had scored from a penalty kick, netting his only goal in the tournament. Following a 1–0 win against defending champions Uruguay, Messi earned his 100th cap for his country in the final group match, a 1–0 win over Jamaica, becoming only the fifth Argentine to achieve this milestone. In his 100 appearances, he had scored a total of 46 goals for Argentina, 22 of which came in official competitive matches.

As Messi evolved from the team's symbolic captain into a genuine leader, he led Argentina to the knockout stage as group winners. In the quarter-final, they created numerous chances, including a rebound header by Messi, but were repeatedly denied by Colombia's goalkeeper, and ultimately ended the match scoreless, leading to a 5–4 penalty shootout in their favour, with Messi netting his team's first spot kick. At the semi-final stage, Messi excelled as a playmaker as he provided three assists and helped create three more goals in his side's 6–1 victory over Paraguay, receiving applause from the initially hostile crowd.

Argentina started the final as the odds-on title favourites, but were defeated by Chile 4–1 in a penalty shootout after a 0–0 extra-time draw. Faced with aggression from opposing players, including taking a boot to the midriff, Messi played below his standards, though he was the only Argentine to successfully convert his penalty. At the close of the tournament, he was reportedly selected to receive the Most Valuable Player award but rejected the honour. As Argentina continued a trophy drought that began in 1993, the World Cup and Copa América defeats again brought intense criticism for Messi from Argentine media and fans.

- **Lionel Messi in 2016–2017 Third Copa América final, retirement, and return**

Messi's place in Argentina's Copa América Centenario squad was initially put in jeopardy when he sustained a back injury in a 1–0 friendly win over Honduras in a pre-Copa América warm-up match on 27 May 2016. It was later reported that he had suffered a deep bruise in his lumbar region. He was later left on the bench in Argentina's 2–1 opening win over defending champions Chile on 6 June due to concerns regarding his fitness. Although Messi was declared match-fit for his nation's second group match against Panama on 10 June, Martino left him on the bench once again; he replaced Augusto Fernández in the 61st minute and subsequently scored a hat-trick in 19 minutes, also starting the play which led to Sergio Agüero's goal, as the match ended in a 5–0 victory, sealing Argentina's place in the quarter-finals of the competition. he was elected man of the match for his performance.

On 18 June, in the quarter-final of the Copa América against Venezuela, Messi produced another man of the match performance, assisting two goals and scoring another in a 4–1 victory, which enabled him to equal Gabriel Batistuta's national record of 54 goals in official international matches. This record was broken three days later when Messi scored a free kick in a 4–0 semi-final win against hosts the United States; he also assisted two goals during the match as Argentina sealed a place in the final of the competition for a second consecutive year, and was named man of the match once again.

During a repeat of the previous year's final on 26 June, Argentina once again lost to Chile on penalties after a 0–0 deadlock, resulting in Messi's third consecutive defeat in a major tournament final with Argentina, and his fourth overall. After the match, Messi, who had missed his penalty in the shootout, announced his retirement from international football. He stated, "I tried my hardest. The team has ended for me, a decision made." Chile coach Juan Antonio Pizzi said after the match, "My generation can't compare him to Maradona that's for my generation, because of what Maradona did for Argentine football. But I think the best player ever played today here in the United States."

Messi finished the tournament as the second highest scorer, behind Eduardo Vargas, with five goals, and was the highest assist provider with four assists, also winning more Man of the Match awards than any other player in the tournament (3).he was named to the team of the tournament for his performances, but missed out on the Golden Ball Award for best player, which went to Alexis Sánchez.

Following his announcement, a campaign began in Argentina for Messi to change his mind about retiring. He was greeted by fans with signs like "Don't go, Leo" when the team landed in Buenos Aires. President of Argentina Mauricio Macri urged Messi not to quit, stating, "We are lucky, it is one of life's pleasures, it is a gift from God to have the best player in the world in a footballing country like ours... Lionel Messi is the greatest thing we have in Argentina and we must take care of him." Mayor of Buenos Aires Horacio Rodríguez Larreta unveiled a statue of Messi in the capital to convince him to reconsider retirement. The campaign also continued in the streets and avenues of the Argentine capital, with about 50,000 supporters going to the Obelisco de Buenos Aires on 2 July, using the same slogan.

Just a week after Messi announced his international retirement, Argentine newspaper La Nación reported that he was reconsidering playing for Argentina at the 2018 FIFA World Cup qualifiers in September. On 12 August, it was confirmed that Messi had reversed his decision to retire from international football, and he was included in the squad for the national team's upcoming 2018 World Cup qualifiers. On 1 September, in his first game back, he scored in a 1–0 home win over Uruguay in a 2018 World Cup qualifier.

Messi celebrates his hat-trick against Ecuador in 2017 which saw Argentina qualify for the 2018 FIFA World Cup.On 28 March 2017, Messi was suspended for four international games for insulting an assistant referee in a game against Chile on 23 March 2017. He was also fined CHF 10,000. On 5 May, Messi's four match ban as well as his 10,000 CHF fine was lifted by FIFA after Argentina Football Association appealed against his suspension, which meant he could now play Argentina's remaining World Cup Qualifiers.

Argentina's place in the 2018 World Cup was in jeopardy going into their final qualifying match as they were sixth in their group, outside the five possible CONMEBOL World Cup qualifying spots, meaning they risked failing to qualify for the World Cup for the first time since 1970. On 10 October, Messi led his country to World Cup qualification in scoring a hat-trick as Argentina came from behind to defeat Ecuador 3–1 away; Argentina had not defeated Ecuador in Quito since 2001. Messi's three goals saw him become the joint all-time leading scorer in CONMEBOL World Cup qualifiers with 21 goals, alongside Uruguay's Luis Suárez, overtaking the previous record which was held by compatriot Hernán Crespo.

• Lionel Messi in 2018 World Cup

"The squad is the worst in their history. Even having the best player in the world was not capable of creating a competitive team. All the decline of recent times was hidden by this unrivalled genius "

Following on from their poor qualification campaign, expectations were not high going into the 2018 World Cup, with the team, without an injured

Messi, losing 6–1 to Spain in March 2018. Prior to Argentina's opener, there was speculation in the media over whether this would be Messi's final World Cup. In the team's opening group match against Iceland on 16 June, Messi missed a potential match-winning penalty in an eventual 1–1 draw. In Argentina's second game on 21 June, the team lost 3–0 to Croatia. Post-match the Argentina coach Jorge Sampaoli spoke of the lack of quality in the team surrounding Messi, saying "we quite simply couldn't pass to him to help him generate the situations he is used to. We worked to give him the ball but the opponent also worked hard to prevent him from getting the ball. We lost that battle". Croatia captain and midfielder Luka Modrić also stated post match, "Messi is an incredible player but he can't do everything alone."

- **Messi celebrates his goal against Nigeria at the 2018 FIFA World Cup**

In Argentina's final group match against Nigeria at the Krestovsky Stadium, Saint Petersburg on 26 June, Messi scored the opening goal in an eventual 2–1 victory, becoming the third Argentine after Diego Maradona and Gabriel Batistuta to score in three different World Cups; he also became the first player to score in the World Cup in his teens, twenties, and his thirties. A goal of the tournament contender, Messi received a long pass from midfield and controlled the ball on the run with two touches before striking it across goal into the net with his weaker right foot. He was awarded Man of the Match.

Argentina progressed to the second round as group runners-up behind Croatia. In the round of 16 match against eventual champions France on 30 June, Messi set up Gabriel Mercado's and Sergio Agüero's goals in a 3–4 defeat, which saw Argentina eliminated from the World Cup. With his two assists in his team's second round fixture, Messi became the first player to provide an assist in the last four World Cups, and also became the first player to provide two assists in a match for Argentina since Maradona had managed the same feat against South Korea in 1986.

Following the tournament, Messi stated that he would not participate in Argentina's friendlies against Guatemala and Colombia in September, and commented that it would be unlikely that he would represent his nation for the remainder of the calendar year. Messi's absence from the national team and his continued failure to win a title with Argentina prompted speculation in the media that Messi might retire from international football once again. In March 2019, however, he was called up to the Argentina squad once again for the team's friendlies against Venezuela and Morocco later that month. A conversation with Scaloni and his idol Aimar made Messi reconsider his decision to retire. He made his international return on 22 March, in a 3–1 friendly defeat to Venezuela, in Madrid.

On 21 May, Messi was included in Lionel Scaloni's final 23-man Argentina squad for the 2019 Copa América. In Argentina's second group match of the tournament on 19 June, Messi scored the equalising goal from the penalty spot in a 1–1 draw against Paraguay. After coming under criticism in the media over his performance following Argentina's 2–0 victory over Venezuela in the quarter-finals at the Maracanã Stadium on 28 June, Messi commented that it had not been his best Copa América, while also criticising the poor quality of the pitches. Following Argentina's 2–0 defeat to hosts Brazil in the semi-finals on 2 July, Messi was critical of the refereeing during the match, and alleged the competition was "set up" for Brazil to win.

In the third-place match against Chile on 6 July, Messi set-up Agüero's opening goal from a free kick in an eventual 2–1 win, to help Argentina capture the bronze medal; however, he was sent off along with Gary Medel in the 37th minute of play, after being involved in an altercation with the Chilean defender. Following the match, Messi refused to collect his medal, and implied in a post-match interview that his comments following the semi-final led to his sending off. Messi later issued an apology for his comments, but was fined $1,500 and was handed a one-match ban by CONMEBOL, which ruled him out of Argentina's next World Cup qualifier.

On 2 August, Messi was banned for three months from international football and was fined $50,000 by CONMEBOL for his comments against the referee's decisions; this ban meant he would miss Argentina's friendly matches against Chile, Mexico and Germany in September and October. On 15 November, Messi played in the 2019 Superclásico de las Américas versus Brazil, scoring the winning goal by a rebound of his saved penalty. On 8 October 2020, Messi scored a penalty in a 1–0 victory against Ecuador, giving Argentina a winning start to their 2022 World Cup qualifying campaign.

- **Lionel Messi in 2021 Copa América win, goal and appearance records**

On 14 June 2021, Messi scored from a free kick in a 1–1 draw against Chile in Argentina's opening group match of the 2021 Copa América in Brazil. On 21 June, Messi played in his 147th match as he equalled Javier

Mascherano's record for most appearances for Argentina in a 1–0 win over Paraguay in their third game of the tournament. A week later, he broke the record for most appearances in an Argentina shirt when he featured in a 4–1 win against Bolivia in his team's final group match, assisting Papu Gómez's opening goal and later scoring two. On 3 July, Messi assisted twice and scored from a free-kick in a 3–0 win over Ecuador in the quarter-finals of the competition.

On 6 July, in a 1–1 draw in the semi-finals against Colombia, Messi made his 150th appearance for his country and registered his fifth assist of the tournament, a cut-back for Lautaro Martínez, matching his record of nine goal contributions in a single tournament from five years earlier; he later netted his spot kick in Argentina's eventual 3–2 penalty shoot-out victory to progress to his fifth international final. On 10 July, Argentina defeated hosts Brazil 1–0 in the final, giving Messi his first major international title and Argentina's first since 1993, as well as his nation's joint record 15th Copa América overall. Messi was directly involved in 9 out of the 12 goals scored by Argentina, scoring four and assisting five; he was named the player of the tournament for his performances, an honour he shared with Neymar. He also finished as the tournament's top scorer with four goals tied with Colombia's Luis Díaz, with the Golden Boot awarded to Messi as he had more assists.

- **Messi at the 2022 FIFA World Cup**

On 9 September, Messi scored a hat-trick in a 3–0 home win over Bolivia in a 2022 World Cup qualifier which also moved him above Pelé as South America's top male international scorer with 79 goals. In the 2022 Finalissima, the third edition of the CONMEBOL–UEFA Cup of Champions, at Wembley on 2 June 2022, Messi assisted twice in a 3–0 victory against Italy and was named player of the match, securing his second trophy for Argentina at the senior level. Messi then followed this on 6 June with all five Argentina goals in a 5–0 victory in a friendly win over Estonia, overtaking Ferenc Puskás among the all-time international men's top scorers.

At the 2022 FIFA World Cup in Qatar, Messi scored a penalty in Argentina's opening game, a 2–1 defeat to Saudi Arabia, before scoring with a low 20-yard strike in their next match against Mexico in which Argentina won 2–0, also recording an assist on Enzo Fernández's goal. In the last 16 game against Australia, Messi scored the opening goal in Argentina's 2–1 win in what was his 1,000[th] senior career appearance, and became the most-capped male South American (CONMEBOL member) footballer of all time, surpassing the previous record set by Ecuador's Iván Hurtado, as well as surpass and equal several other FIFA World Cup and national team records.

In the quarter-final against the Netherlands, Messi assisted Argentina's first goal for Nahuel Molina with a reverse pass and then scored a penalty as the game finished 2–2 after extra time. Argentina won 4–3 in the penalty shootout, with Messi scoring the first penalty. In the semi-final against Croatia, Messi made a record-equalling 25th World Cup finals appearance, drawing level with Germany's Lothar Matthäus, and scored the opening goal with a penalty before he assisted Argentina's third goal scored by Julián Álvarez in a 3–0 win with his 11th World Cup goal, he overtook Batistuta to become Argentina's all–time top–scorer at the World Cup. Argentina advanced to the final against France, with Messi stating that it would be his final World Cup appearance.

In the 2022 FIFA World Cup final on 18 December, Messi made his record 26th World Cup finals appearance at Lusail Stadium. Messi scored Argentina's opening goal with a penalty, becoming in the process the first player since the last-16 round was introduced in 1986 to score a goal in each round of a single World Cup edition. After Argentina's eventual two-goal lead was erased by France forward Kylian Mbappé who scored twice inside two minutes, Messi would score again in extra-time to restore Argentina's lead, before Mbappé drew France level. Tied 3–3 after extra-time, the match went to a penalty shoot-out. Messi scored Argentina's first goal in the shoot-out, with Argentina eventually winning 4–2, ending the nation's 36-year wait for the trophy.

Messi received the Golden Ball for player of the tournament, becoming the first player to win it twice. He finished second in the Golden Boot race with seven goals in seven games, one behind Mbappé. With his appearance and brace in the final, Messi overtook Matthäus as the player with most appearances at the World Cup (26), and Pelé as the player with most direct goal contributions at the World Cup since 1966 (21 – 13 goals and 8 assists). The championship game was widely acclaimed as one of the best of all time, with media coverage heavily framing it as a duel between Messi and Mbappé. Following the game, Messi confirmed that he had no plans to retire from the national team, saying "I want to continue playing as a champion."

- **Lionel Messi Style of play**

Due to his short stature, Messi has a lower centre of gravity than taller players, which gives him greater agility, allowing him to change direction more quickly and evade opposing tackles. this has led the Spanish media to dub him La Pulga Atómica . Despite being physically unimposing, he possesses significant upper-body strength, which, combined with his low centre of gravity and resulting balance, aids him in withstanding physical challenges from opponents; he has consequently been noted for his lack of diving in a sport rife with playacting. His short, strong legs allow him to excel in short bursts of acceleration while his quick feet enable him to retain control of the ball when dribbling at speed. His former Barcelona manager Pep Guardiola once stated, "Messi is the only player that runs faster with the ball than he does without it." Although he has improved his ability with his weaker foot since his mid-20s, Messi is predominantly a left-footed player; with the outside of his left foot, he usually begins dribbling runs, while he uses the inside of his foot to finish and provide passes and assists.

A prolific goalscorer, Messi is known for his finishing, positioning, quick reactions, and ability to make attacking runs to beat the defensive line. He also functions in a playmaking role, courtesy of his vision and range of passing.He has often been described as a magician; a conjurer, creating goals and opportunities where seemingly none exist. Moreover, he is an accurate free kick and penalty kick taker. As of October 2022, Messi ranks 9th all time in goals scored from direct free kicks with 60, the most among active players. He also has a penchant for scoring from chips.Messi is known to drop deep, link-up with midfielders, orchestrate attacking plays, and create goal-scoring opportunities.

Messi's pace and technical ability enable him to undertake individual dribbling runs towards goal, in particular during counterattacks, usually starting from the halfway line or the right side of the pitch. Widely considered to be the best dribbler in the world, and one of the greatest dribblers of all time, with regard to this ability, his former Argentina manager Diego Maradona has said of him, "The ball stays glued to his foot; I've seen great players in my career, but I've never seen anyone with Messi's ball control." Beyond his individual qualities, he is also a well-rounded, hard-working team player, known for his creative combinations, in particular with former Barcelona midfielders Xavi and Andrés Iniesta.

Tactically, Messi plays in a free attacking role; a versatile player, he is capable of attacking on either wing or through the centre of the pitch. His favoured position in childhood was the playmaker behind two strikers, known as the enganche in Argentine football, but he began his career in Spain as a left-winger or left-sided forward. Upon his first-team debut, he was moved onto the right wing by manager Frank Rijkaard; from this position, he could more easily cut through the defence into the middle of the pitch and curl shots on goal with his left foot, rather than predominantly cross balls for teammates. Under Guardiola and subsequent managers, he most often played in a false nine role; positioned as a centre-forward or lone striker, he would roam the centre, often moving deep into midfield and drawing defenders with him, in order to create and exploit spaces for passes, other teammates' attacking runs off the ball, Messi's own dribbling runs, or combinations with Xavi and Iniesta.

Under the stewardship of Luis Enrique, Messi initially returned to playing in the right-sided position that characterised much of his early career in the manager's 4–3–3 formation, while he was increasingly deployed in a deeper, free playmaking role in later seasons. Under manager Ernesto Valverde, Messi played in a variety of roles. While he occasionally continued to be deployed in a deeper role, from which he could make runs from behind into the box, or even on the right wing or as a false nine, he was also used in a more offensive, central role in a 4–2–3–1, or as a second striker in a 4–4–2 formation, where he was once again given the licence to drop deep, link-up with midfielders, orchestrate his team's attacking plays, and create chances for his attacking partner Suárez.

- **Messi prepares to shoot with his dominant left foot in the 2014 FIFA World Cup Final**

As his career advanced, and his tendency to dribble diminished slightly with age, Messi began to dictate play in deeper areas of the pitch and developed into one of the best passers and playmakers in football history.

His work-rate off the ball and defensive responsibilities also decreased as his career progressed; by covering less ground on the pitch, and instead conserving his energy for short bursts of speed, he was able to improve his efficiency, movement, and positional play, and was also able to avoid muscular injuries, despite often playing a large number of matches throughout a particular season on a consistent basis. Indeed, while he was injury-prone in his early career, he was later able to improve his injury record by running less off the ball, and by adopting a stricter diet, training regime, and sleep schedule. With the Argentina national team, Messi has similarly played anywhere along the frontline; under various managers, he has been employed on the right wing, as a false nine, as an out-and-out striker, in a supporting role alongside another forward, or in a deeper, free creative role as a classic number 10 playmaker or attacking midfielder behind the strikers.

A prodigious talent as a teenager, Messi established himself among the world's best players before age 20. Diego Maradona considered the 18-year-old Messi the best player in the world alongside Ronaldinho, while the Brazilian himself, shortly after winning the Ballon d'Or, commented, "I'm not even the best at Barça", in reference to his protégé. Four years later, after Messi had won his first Ballon d'Or by a record margin, the public debate regarding his qualities as a player moved beyond his status in contemporary football to the possibility that he was one of the greatest players in history.

An early proponent was his then-manager Pep Guardiola, who, as early as August 2009, declared Messi to be the best player he had ever seen. In the following years, this opinion gained greater acceptance among pundits, managers, former and current players, and by the end of Barça's second treble-winning season, Messi's superiority, ahead of Maradona and Pelé, had become the apparent view among many fans and pundits in continental Europe. He initially received several dismissals by critics, based on the fact that he had not won an international trophy at senior level with Argentina, until he won his first at the 2021 Copa América.

Throughout his career, Messi has been compared with his late compatriot Diego Maradona, due to their similar playing styles as diminutive, left-footed dribblers. Initially, he was merely one of many young Argentine players, including his boyhood idol Pablo Aimar, to receive the "New Maradona" moniker, but as his career progressed, Messi proved his similarity beyond all previous contenders, establishing himself as the greatest player Argentina had produced since Maradona. Jorge Valdano, who won the 1986 World Cup alongside Maradona, said in October 2013, "Messi is Maradona every day. For the last five years, Messi has been the Maradona of the World Cup in Mexico." César Menotti, who as manager orchestrated their 1978 World Cup victory, echoed this sentiment when he opined that Messi plays "at the level of the best Maradona". Other notable Argentines in the sport, such as Osvaldo Ardiles, Javier Zanetti, and Diego Simeone, have expressed their belief that Messi has overtaken Maradona as the best player in history.

In Argentine society, prior to 2019, Messi was generally held in lesser esteem than Maradona, a consequence of not only his perceived uneven performances with the national team, but also of differences in class, personality, and background. Messi is in some ways the antithesis of his predecessor: where Maradona was an extroverted, controversial character who rose to greatness from the slums, Messi is reserved and unassuming, an unremarkable man outside of football. An enduring mark against him is the fact that, through no fault of his own, he never proved himself in the Argentine Primera División as an upcoming player, achieving stardom overseas from a young age, while his lack of outward passion for the Albiceleste shirt have in the past led to the false perception that he felt Catalan rather than truly Argentine.

Football journalist Tim Vickery states the view among Argentines is that Messi "was always seen as more Catalan than one of them". Despite having lived in Spain since age 13, Messi rejected the option of representing Spain internationally. He has said: "Argentina is my country, my family, my way of expressing myself. I would change all my records to make the people in my country happy." Moreover, several pundits and footballing figures, including Maradona, questioned Messi's leadership with Argentina at times, despite his playing ability. Vickery states the perception of Messi among Argentines changed in 2019, with Messi making a conscious effort to become "more one of the group, more Argentine", with Vickery adding that following the World Cup victory in 2022 Messi would now be held in the same esteem by his compatriots as Maradona.

- ## Messi–Ronaldo rivalry

Among his contemporary peers, Messi is most often compared and contrasted with Portuguese forward Cristiano Ronaldo, as part of an ongoing rivalry that has been compared to past sports rivalries like the Muhammad Ali–Joe Frazier rivalry in boxing, the Roger Federer–Rafael Nadal rivalry in tennis, and the Senna–Prost rivalry from Formula One motor racing.

Although Messi has at times denied any rivalry, they are widely believed to push one another in their aim to be the best player in the world. Since 2008, Messi has won seven Ballons d'Or to Ronaldo's five, six FIFA World's Best Player awards to Ronaldo's five, and six European Golden Shoes to Ronaldo's four. Pundits and fans regularly argue the individual merits of both players. Beyond their playing styles, the debate also revolves around their differing physiques – Ronaldo is 1.87 m (6 ft 1+1⁄2 in) with a muscular build – and contrasting public personalities with Ronaldo's self-confidence and theatrics a foil to Messi's humility. From 2009–10 to 2017–18, Messi faced Ronaldo at least twice every season in El Clásico, which ranks among the world's most viewed annual sports events. Off the pitch, Ronaldo is his direct competitor in terms of salary, sponsorships, and social media fanbase.

- **Lionel Messi In popular culture**

According to France Football, Messi was the world's highest-paid footballer for five years out of six between 2009 and 2014; he was the first player to exceed the 40 million benchmark, with earnings of €41 million in 2013, and the 50–60 million points, with income of 65 million in 2014. Messi was second on Forbes list of the world's highest-paid athletes with income of $81.4 million from his salary and endorsements in 2015–16. In 2018 he was the first player to exceed the €100m benchmark for a calendar year, with earnings of 126m (154m) in combined income from salaries, bonuses and endorsements.

Forbes ranked him the world's highest-paid athlete in 2019. From 2008, he was Barcelona's highest-paid player, receiving a salary that increased incrementally from 7.8 million to €13 million over the next five years. Signing a new Barcelona contract in 2017, he earned $667,000 per week in wages, and Barcelona also paid him $59.6 million as a signing on bonus. His buyout clause was set at $835 million (€700 million). In 2020, Messi became the second footballer, as well as the second athlete in a team sport, after Cristiano Ronaldo, to surpass $1 billion in earnings during their careers.

In addition to his salary and bonuses, much of his income derives from endorsements; SportsPro has consequently cited him as one of the world's most marketable athletes every year since their research began in 2010. His main sponsor since 2006 is the sportswear company Adidas. As Barcelona's leading youth prospect, he had been signed with Nike since age 14, but transferred to Adidas after they successfully challenged their rival's claim to his image rights in court. Over time, Messi established himself as their leading brand endorser from 2008, he had a long-running signature collection of Adidas F50 boots, and in 2015, he became the first footballer to receive his own sub-brand of Adidas boots, the Adidas Messi. Since 2017, he has worn the latest version of the Adidas Nemeziz. In 2015, a Barcelona jersey with Messi's name and number was the best-selling replica jersey worldwide.

After blessing himself, Messi often celebrates a goal by pointing a finger on each hand towards the sky in dedication to his late grandmother. His goal celebration features in the FIFA video game series, first appearing in FIFA 14.

As a commercial entity, Messi's marketing brand has been based exclusively on his talents and achievements as a player, in contrast to arguably more glamorous players like Cristiano Ronaldo and David Beckham. At the start of his career, he thus mainly held sponsorship contracts with companies that employ sports-oriented marketing, such as Adidas, Pepsi, and Konami. From 2010 onwards, concurrently with his increased achievements as a player, his marketing appeal widened, leading to long-term endorsement deals with luxury brands Dolce & Gabbana and Audemars Piguet. Messi is also a global brand ambassador for Gillette, Turkish Airlines, Ooredoo, and Tata Motors, among other companies. Additionally, Messi was the face of Konami's video game series Pro Evolution Soccer, appearing on the covers of PES 2009, PES 2010, PES 2011 and PES 2020. He subsequently signed with rival company EA Sports to become the face of their series FIFA and has since appeared on four consecutive covers from FIFA 13 to FIFA 16.

Messi's global popularity and influence are well documented. He was among the Time 100, an annual list of the world's most influential people as published by Time, in 2011 and 2012. His fanbase on the social media website Facebook is among the largest of all public figures: within seven hours of its launch in April 2011, Messi's Facebook page had nearly seven million followers, and by August 2021 he had over 103 million followers, the second highest for a sportsperson after Cristiano Ronaldo. He also has over 400 million Instagram followers, the second highest for an individual and sportsperson after Cristiano Ronaldo. According to a 2014 survey by sports research firm Repucom in 15 international markets, Messi was familiar to 87% of respondents around the world, of whom 78% perceived him favourably, making him the second-most recognised player globally, behind Ronaldo, and the most likable of all contemporary players. On Messi's economic impact on the city in which he plays, Terry Gibson called him a "tourist attraction".

· **Indian vehicle art of Messi**

Other events have illustrated Messi's presence in popular culture. A solid gold replica of his left foot, weighing 25 kg (55 lb) and valued at $5.25 million, went on sale in Japan in March 2013 to raise funds for victims of the 2011 Tōhoku earthquake and tsunami. A 2013 Turkish Airlines advertisement starring Messi, in which he engages in a selfie competition with then-Los Angeles Lakers star Kobe Bryant, was the most-watched ad on YouTube in the year of its release, receiving 137 million views, and was subsequently voted the best advertisement of the 2005–15 decade to commemorate YouTube's founding. World Press Photo selected "The Final Game", a photograph of Messi facing the World Cup trophy after Argentina's final defeat to Germany, as the best sports image of 2014. Messi, a documentary about his life by filmmaker Álex de la Iglesia, premiered at the Venice Film Festival in August 2014.

In June 2021, Messi signed a five-year deal to become an ambassador for the Hard Rock Cafe brand. He stated, "sports and music are an integral part of my life. It is an honor to be the first athlete to partner with a brand who has a history of teaming with music legends." In May 2022, Messi was unveiled as Saudi Arabia's tourism ambassador. Due to Saudi Arabia's poor human rights record, Messi was condemned for taking on the role which was viewed as an attempt of Saudi sportswashing. In August 2022, Messi was urged by the family of Mohammed al Faraj to intervene on their son's behalf after he was arrested in 2017 at the age of 15 for crimes against the Saudi regime and faced the death penalty.

- **Lionel Messi Personal life**

Since 2008, Messi has been in a relationship with Antonela Roccuzzo, a fellow native of Rosario. He has known Roccuzzo since he was five years old, as she is the cousin of his childhood best friend, Lucas Scaglia, who is also a football player. After keeping their relationship private for a year, Messi first confirmed their romance in an interview in January 2009, before going public a month later during a carnival in Sitges after the Barcelona–Espanyol derby.

Messi and Roccuzzo have three sons: Thiago (born 2012), Mateo (born 2015) and Ciro (born 2018). To celebrate his partner's first pregnancy, Messi placed the ball under his shirt after scoring in Argentina's 4–0 win against Ecuador on 2 June 2012, before confirming the pregnancy in an interview two weeks later. Thiago was born in Barcelona on 2 November 2012. In

April 2015, Messi confirmed that they were expecting another child. On 30 June 2017, he married Roccuzzo at a luxury hotel named Hotel City Center in Rosario. In October 2017, his wife announced they were expecting their third child. Messi and his family are Catholic Christians.

Messi enjoys a close relationship with his immediate family members, particularly his mother, Celia, whose face he has tattooed on his left shoulder. His professional affairs are largely run as a family business: his father, Jorge, has been his agent since he was 14, and his oldest brother, Rodrigo, handles his daily schedule and publicity. His mother and other brother, Matías, manage his charitable organization, the Leo Messi Foundation, and take care of personal and professional matters in Rosario.

Since leaving for Spain aged 13, Messi has maintained close ties to his hometown of Rosario, even preserving his distinct Rosarino accent. He has kept ownership of his family's old house, although it has long stood empty; he maintains a penthouse apartment in an exclusive residential building for his mother, as well as a family compound just outside the city. Once when he was in training with the national team in Buenos Aires, he made a three-hour trip by car to Rosario immediately after practice to have dinner with his family, spent the night with them, and returned to Buenos Aires the next day in time for practice

. Messi keeps in daily contact via phone and text with a small group of confidants in Rosario, most of whom were fellow members of "The Machine of '87" at Newell's Old Boys. He currently lives in Castelldefels, a village near Barcelona. He was on bad terms with the club after his transfer to Barcelona, but by 2012 their public feud had ended, with Newell's embracing their ties with Messi, even issuing a club membership card to his newborn son. Messi has long planned to return to Rosario to end his playing career at Newell's. Messi holds triple citizenship, as he is a citizen of Argentina, Italy, and Spain.

Throughout his career, Messi has been involved in charitable efforts aimed at vulnerable children, a commitment that stems in part from the medical difficulties he faced in his own childhood. Since 2004, he has contributed his time and finances to the United Nations Children's Fund (UNICEF), an organisation with which Barcelona also have a strong association.

Messi has served as a UNICEF goodwill ambassador since his appointment in March 2010, completing his first field mission for the organisation four months later as he travelled to Haiti to bring public awareness to the plight of the country's children in the wake of the recent earthquake. He has since participated in UNICEF campaigns targeting HIV prevention, education, and the social inclusion of disabled children. To celebrate his son's first birthday, in November 2013, Messi and Thiago were part of a publicity campaign to raise awareness of mortality rates among disadvantaged children.

In addition to his work with UNICEF, Messi founded his own charitable organisation, the Leo Messi Foundation, which supports access to health care, education, and sport for children. It was established in 2007 following a visit Messi paid to a hospital for terminally ill children in Boston, an experience that resonated with him to the point that he decided to reinvest part of his earnings into society. Through his foundation, Messi has awarded research grants, financed medical training, and invested in the development of medical centres and projects in Argentina, Spain, and elsewhere in the world. In addition to his own fundraising activities, such as his global "Messi and Friends" football matches, his foundation receives financial support from various companies to which he has assigned his name in endorsement agreements, with Adidas as their main sponsor.

Messi has also invested in youth football in Argentina: he financially supports Sarmiento, a football club based in the Rosario neighbourhood where he was born, committing in 2013 to the refurbishment of their facilities and the installation of all-weather pitches, and funds the management of several youth players at Newell's Old Boys and rival club Rosario Central, as well as at River Plate and Boca Juniors in Buenos Aires. At Newell's Old Boys, his boyhood club, he funded the 2012 construction of a new gymnasium and a dormitory inside the club's stadium for their youth academy. His former youth coach at Newell's, Ernesto Vecchio, is employed by the Leo Messi Foundation as a talent scout for young players. On 7 June 2016, Messi won a libel case against La Razón newspaper and was awarded €65,000 in damages, which he donated to the charity Médecins Sans Frontières. Messi made a donation worth €1 million ($1.1 million) to fight the spread of coronavirus.

This was split between Clinic Barcelona hospital in Barcelona, Spain and his native Argentina.[626] In addition to this, Messi along with his fellow FC Barcelona teammates announced he will be taking a 70% cut in salaries during the 2020 coronavirus emergency, and contribute further to the club to provide fully to salaries of all the clubs employees.

In November 2016, with the Argentine Football Association being run by a FIFA committee for emergency due to an economic crisis, it was reported that three of the national team's security staff told Messi that they had not received their salaries for six months. He stepped in and paid the salaries of the three members. In February 2021, Messi donated to the Museu Nacional d'Art de Catalunya his Adidas shoes which he wore when he scored his 644th goal for Barcelona and broke Pelé's record for most goals scored for a single club; the shoes were later auctioned off in April by the museum for charity to help children with cancer and were sold for £125,000.

In advance of the 2021 Copa América in Uruguay, Messi donated three signed shirts to the Chinese pharmaceutical firm Sinovac Biotech—whose directors spoke of their admiration for Messi—in order to secure 50,000 doses of Sinovac's COVID-19 vaccine, CoronaVac, in the hope of vaccinating all of South America's football players. A deal brokered by Uruguay's president Luis Lacalle Pou, the plan to prioritise football players caused some controversy given widespread vaccine scarcity in the region, with the Mayor of Canelones in Uruguay remarking that "Just as the president manifested cooperation with CONMEBOL to vaccinate for the Copa América, he could just as well have the same consideration for Canelones".

Messi's financial affairs came under investigation in 2013 for suspected tax evasion. Offshore companies in tax havens Uruguay and Belize were used to evade €4.1 million in taxes related to sponsorship earnings between 2007 and 2009. An unrelated shell company in Panama set up in 2012 was subsequently identified as belonging to the Messis in the Panama Papers data leak. Messi, who pleaded ignorance of the alleged scheme, voluntarily paid arrears of €5.1 million in August 2013. On 6 July 2016, Messi and his father were both found guilty of tax fraud and were handed suspended 21-month prison sentences and respectively ordered to pay €1.7 million and €1.4 million in fines. Facing the judge, he said, "I just played football. I signed the contracts because I trusted my dad and the lawyers and we had decided that they would take charge of those things.

TWO

THE HISTORY OF FOOTBALL

Football (or soccer as the game is called in some parts of the world) has a long history. Football in its current form arose in England in the middle of the 19th century. But alternative versions of the game existed much earlier and are a part of the football history.

- **history and the precursors of football**

The first known examples of a team game involving a ball, which was made out of a rock, occurred in old Mesoamerican cultures for over 3,000 years ago. It was by the Aztecs called Tchatali, although various versions of the game were spread over large regions. In some ritual occasions, the ball would symbolize the sun and the captain of the losing team would be sacrificed to the gods. A unique feature of the Mesoamerican ball game versions was a bouncing ball made of rubber – no other early culture had access to rubber.

The first known ball game which also involved kicking took place In China in the 3rd and 2nd century BC under the name cuju. Cuju was played with a round ball (stitched leather with fur or feathers inside) on an area of a square. A modified form of this game later spread to Japan and was by the name of kemari practiced under ceremonial forms.

Perhaps even older cuju was Marn Gook, played by Aboriginal Australians and according to white emigrants in the 1800s a ball game primarily involving kicking. The ball was made by encased leaves or roots. The rules are mostly unknown, but as with many other early versions of the game keeping the ball in the air was probably a chief feature.

Other variety of ball games had been known from Ancient Greece. The ball was made by shreds of leather filled with hair (the first documents of balls filled with air are from the 7th century). Ball games had, however, a low status and was not included at the Panhellenic Games. In the Ancient Rome, games with balls were not included in the entertainment on the big arenas (amphitheaters), but occurred in exercises in the military by the name of Harpastum. It was the Roman culture that would bring football to the British island (Britannica). It is, however, uncertain in which degree the British people were influenced by this variety and in which degree they had developed their own variants.

· **The game of football takes its form**

The most admitted story tells that the game was developed in England in the 12th century. In this century, games that resembled football were played on meadows and roads in England. Besides from kicks, the game involved also punches of the ball with the fist. This early form of football was also much more rough and violent than the modern way of playing.

An important feature of the forerunners to football was that the games involved plenty of people and took place over large areas in towns (an equivalent was played in Florence from the 16th century where it was called Calcio). The rampage of these games would cause damage on the town and sometimes death to the participants. These would be among the reasons for the proclamations against the game that finally was forbidden for several centuries. But the football-like games would return to the streets of London in the 17th century. It would be forbidden again in 1835, but at this stage the game had been established in the public schools.

It took, however, long time until the features of today's football had been taken into practice. For a long time there was no clear distinction between football and rugby. There were also many variations concerning the size of the ball, the number of players and the length of a match.

The game was often played in schools and two of the predominant schools were Rugby and Eton. At Rugby the rules included the possibility to take up the ball with the hands and the game we today know as rugby has its origin from here. At Eton on the other hand the ball was played exclusively with the feet and this game can be seen as a close predecessor to the modern football. The game in Rugby was called "the running game" while the game in Eton was called "the dribbling game".

An attempt to create proper rules for the game was done at a meeting in Cambridge in 1848, but a final solution to all questions of rules was not achieved. Another important event in the history of football came about in 1863 in London when the first Football association was formed in England. It was decided that carrying the ball with the hands wasn't allowed. The meeting also resulted in a standardization of the size and weight of the ball. A consequence of the London meeting was that the game was divided into two codes: association football and rugby.

The game would, however, continue to develop for a long time and there was still much flexibility concerning the rules. For one thing, the number of players on the pitch could vary. Neither were uniforms used to distinguish the appearance of the teams. It was also common with players wearing caps – the header was yet to be a part of the game yet. Further reading: The development of football rules.

Another important difference at this stage could be noticed between English and Scottish teams. Whereas the English teams preferred to run forward with the ball in a more rugby fashion, the Scottish chose to pass the ball between their players. It would be the Scottish approach that soon became predominant.

The sport was at first an entertainment for the British working class. Unprecedented amounts of spectators, up to 30,000, would see the big matches in the late 19th century. The game would soon expand by British peoples who traveled to other parts of the world. Especially in South America and India would the interest in football become big.

· **The first football clubs**

Football clubs have existed since the 15th century, but unorganized and without official status. It is therefore hard to decide which the first football club was. Some historians suggest that it was the Foot-Ball Club formed 1824 in Edinburgh. Early clubs were often formed by former school students and the first of this kind was formed in Sheffield in 1855. The oldest among professional football clubs is the English club Notts County that was formed in 1862 and still exists today.

An important step for the emergence of teams was the industrialization that led to larger groups of people meeting at places such as factories, pubs and churches. Football teams were established in the larger cities and the new railroads could bring them to other cities.In the beginning, football was dominated by public school teams, but later, teams consisting by workers would make up the majority. Another change was successively taking place when some clubs became willing to pay the best players to join their team. This would be the start of a long period of transition, not without friction, in which the game would develop to a professional level.

The motivation behind paying players was not only to win more matches. In the 1880s the interest in the game has moved ahead to a level that tickets were sold to the matches. And finally, in 1885 professional football was legalized and three years later the Football League was established. During the first season, 12 clubs joined the league, but soon more clubs became interested and the competition would consequently expand into more divisions.For a long time, the British teams would be dominant. After some decades, clubs from Prague, Budapest and Sienna would be the primarily contenders to the British dominance.

As with many things in history, women were for a long time excluded from participating in games. It was not before the late 19th century that women started to play football. The first official women's game took place in Inverness in 1888.

· **The first competitions**

Other milestones were now to follow. Football Association Challenge Cup (FA Cup) became the first important competition when it was run in 1871. The following year a match between two national teams was played for the first time. The match that involved England and Scotland ended 0-0 and was followed by 4,000 people at Hamilton Crescent (the picture shows illustrations from this occasion).

Twelve years later, in 1883, the first international tournament took place and included four national teams: England, Ireland, Scotland and

Wales.Football was for a long time a British phenomenon, but it gradually spread to other European countries. The first game that took place outside Europe occurred in Argentina in 1867, but it was foreign British workers who were involved and not Argentinean citizens.

The Fédération Internationale de Football Association (FIFA) was founded in 1904 and a foundation act was signed by representatives from France, Belgium, Denmark, the Netherlands, Spain, Sweden and Switzerland. England and the other British countries did not join FIFA from the start, they had invented the game and saw no reason to subordinate to an association. Still, they joined in the following year, but would not partake in the World Cup until 1950.

Domestic leagues occurred in many countries. The first was, as already mentioned, the English Football League which was established in 1888. The leagues would by time expand by more divisions, which were based on team performance.In 1908 would football for the first time be included as an official sport in the Olympic Games. Until the first FIFA World Cup was played in 1930, the Olympic Games football tournament would rank as the most prestigious on a national level. Women's football was not added until 1996.

· **Black players**

As in many other sports the white male was predominant for a long time. In football black players started being present relatively early and in comparison with, for example, tennis, football has traditionally been known as a sport with a mix of black and white players.In Britain, Andrew Watson is known to be the first black player, and he played in the Scottish club Queen's Park in the 1880s.

· **A game of passion**

Few other sports show examples of passion to that extent as football. The arenas are flocked by shearing people and in front of television even more are watching carefully and sometimes with great enthusiasm. Already in the late 19th century, Goodison Park was built in England in purpose of hosting football games. In 1894, the FA Cup final between Notts County and Bolton Wanderers was attended by 37,000 people. A milestone in the development of football stadiums is the construction of Maracanã Stadium. In the year of 1950 the imposing stadium in Rio de Janeiro was ready for almost 200,000 people. No other sport has seen stadiums of that capacity built to host its games.

There have been two different traditions of fan culture on the arenas: the British and the South American. The British fans adopted the tradition of singing, the repertoire was inspired from pub and working songs among other areas. The South Americans on the other hand would adopt the carnival style which included firecrackers and fireworks, and also the modern phenomena of Bengali fires. Fans in other countries have later adopted a mixture of these traditions.

- **The great modern competitions**

No other sport event besides the Summer Olympic Games can today measure itself with the FIFA World Cup. The first edition of the FIFA World Cup was played in 1930 in Uruguay and has since then returned every fourth year (with two exceptions due to the Second World War). In 1991 the first World Cup for women was held in China and has since then also returned every fourth year.Today the biggest global tournament for clubs is the Champions League (played since 1992), the former European Cup (1955–1991).

- **Globalization of the biggest sport in the world**

In the late 19th century, only a few national football teams existed; England and Scotland had the first active teams that played games against each other in the 1870s. Today there are 211 national associations included in the Fédération Internationale de Football Association (FIFA), the world governing body of the sport. Another proof of the globalization could be seen in the increase of nations participating in the World Cup qualifiers: from 32 in 1934 to over 200 in 2014.

The world regions have been divided into six confederations: Confédération Africaine de Football (CAF), Asian Football Confederation (AFC), Union des Associations Européennes de Football (UEFA), The Confederation of North, Central America and Caribbean Association Football (CONCACAF), Oceania Football Confederation (OFC), and Confederación Sudamericana de Fútbol

(CONMEBOL).

· History of football stadiums

Sport activities elicit fervent responses from people and the passion of players matches the excitement of spectators and fans. The global sporting industry is worth over $600 billion and with the amount of money circulating, major sport arenas boast impressive structures. Speaking of architecture some are more remarkable than others. But, how did football stadiums look originally? How did they evolve? Who are the individuals who changed the pitches from the set aside grass areas to properly maintained stadiums?

· The first stadiums

When Association Football was in its starting phase, people played their matches on spare playing fields, mostly within the public parks. The biggest worry of players was whether passers would understand exactly what was happening and have the courage to walk around the pitch.

With growth of football popularity and professionalism, the need to develop better grounds where players would like to be arose. Football clubs started doing more than just brushing some debris off the grass and sending boys out for short matches. Ground that could be used for football and other games, like rugby, had existed for a while. The very first ground, Sandygate Road, opened already in 1804. Almost 60 years later, the first football match between Hallam and Sheffield FC was played here.

Initially, the markings seen on the local pitches were non-existent. Football pitches featured bollard or fence along the field edges to help players know where they could not go beyond and to keep the spectators closer. In addition to that, the fields featured two sticks, fundamentally, at each pitch end to represent the goals.

It might seem strange to hear that football pitches were the suitable looking grassy areas. In most cases, it was the ideal section of the public park – the straightest part. As the popularity of this game increased, teams started using private land. For example, Preston North End moved in 1875 to Deepdale to play its matches on a ground that was formerly a farm, and considering the initial state of the field, they encountered numerous problems.

- **Dunstable Road, the home for Luton Town FC 1897-1905.**

The period 1889-1910 marked a start of an era of numerous stadium constructions in England; fifty league clubs moved to new stadiums during this period. The stadiums were commonly built in centrum city areas - a circumstance that have created difficulties when the need for an expansion has arose much later.
The stadiums were relatively alike from an architectural aspect. They featured one or two covered grandstand and open terraces was filling out the rest of the oval form around the field.

The overcrowded stands in the late 19th centuries were a proof of the increased interest for the sport in England. In the early 20th century, enormous crowds were gathered in special occasions as finals in competitions. One such occasion was the 1913 FA Cup final played at Crystal Palace with over 120,000 spectators. The overcrowded stands would lead to the first recorded stadium disaster, which happened in 1902 when parts of a stand at Ibrox Park in Glasgow collapsed. The outcome was 25 killed and more than 500 injured. Football historian David Goldblatt writes in The Ball is Round: "The Ibrox disaster was driven by combination of enormous crowds, and a commercialism that sanctioned under-investment in shoddy infrastructure."

- **Development of football stadiums**

Before 1960, football pitches featured regular grass. Later in the 1980s, developers installed drainage systems in them. Originally, pitches required substantial amount of maintenance to keep them in the right shape. They were reliant on regular lighting and watering.

In the year 1958, people witnessed undersoil heating put underneath the football-playing surface in Goodison Park. The twenty miles – roughly thirty kilometers – wire was laid under the surface, costing the football club over £16,000. The purpose of this heating system was to prevent freezing on the pitch and was more effective than the installers thought. And because the ancient drainage system could not cope with the new water floods, the pitch was taken up and relaid in 1960 and better drainage systems installed.

Still, in the year 1960, people witnessed the introduction of first-generation artificial turf. The first-generation artificial turf was very different from the pleasant lifelike artificial grass on soccer pitches today. It was low-piles, stiff nylon fibers attached to asphalt or concrete bases. It was first installed in Astrodome Texas. Professional footballers encountered artificial turf when Luton Town, Queens Park Rangers, Oldham Athletic and Preston North End introduced the second-generation turf to their fields in the year 1980. The United Kingdom government illegalized artificial turf in the year 1995.

· **The modern football stadiums**

In the year 2001, UEFA and FIFA started quality assurance programs for artificial turf development. That helped them come up with industry standards for its use in the soccer world. And as a result, the International Football Association Board tackled the problem of turf in the 2004 Laws of The Game.

4G pitches, also known as fourth generation pitches, came into being in the year 2010 and their popularity has been growing. The pitches are a hybrid of natural grass and artificial turf and people can therefore use them for a very long time without any sign of wear and tear. The increased popularity of turf results from the improved image of The John Smith's Stadium in Huddersfield.

Deesso Grassmaster pitches are now common in our stadiums, but were laid for the first time in 1996 in the home of Huddersfield Giants Rugby League Club and Huddersfield Town Football Club. The benefits of artificial and real turf hybrid are clear. Maintenance problems that were common in earlier days are no longer a big problem. Football pitches are not lit or watered regularly and groundskeepers can easily monitor them.

Football arenas such as Camp Nou in Barcelona, gives the sport events another dimension by their grandiose and spectacular framing.The stadiums have grown bigger and bigger, but on the same time the maximum attendances have decreased. The shift from standing places to seats has increase the safety a lot, but it also means that some old records, such as the

173,850 (unofficially, the attendance has been estimated to be over 200,000), at the Maracanã stadium the 16 July when Brazil played against Uruguay in 1950 World Cup will probably never be broken.

The shift to all-seater stadiums was a result of the Hillsborough disaster in 1989. A regulation stipulated that standing places should be removed completely on all Premier League venues before the start of the 1994-95 season. The same rules have been introduced in several other countries. FIFA and UEFA command nowadays all-seater stadiums for all their competitions.

- ## The economic impact of stadium capacity

The size of a football club's stadiums also reflects the revenues. A team with 30,000 capacity has a major handicap against a team with 60,000 capacity. The latter team can afford bigger players transfers and player wages. In Premier League, Manchester United's Old Trafford was for a long time superior to Arsenal's Highbury in this aspect. Arsenal though the disadvantage was enough critical to invest almost £400 million in a new stadium, which was the Emirates stadium that was ready in 2006. The same route was chosen by Tottenham. White Heart Lane had been their home for over a century, but the revenues from its 36,284 capacity couldn't match that of the other English top clubs. The solution was a gigantic investment that resulted in a plus 60,000 capacity stadium with a removable turf field.

A third factor, besides the amounts of fans that can be capsuled and the revenue aspects, is the symbolic and commercial value. A stadium is an important symbol for the team and when a new stadium is built it should look impressive. In many ways ... as Joshua Robinson and Jonathan Clegg puts it in The Club: "Arsenal's new stadium wouldn't just be a venue for 60,000 fans attending in person, it would be a backdrop for the 60 million watching around the world".Tottenham Hotspur Stadium is hard to miss if you are in the neighborhood.

Football stadiums gets enormous media exposure, which has opened win-win situations for owners and other companies. Several clubs have profited by given naming rights to companies that is willing to pay for the branding opportunity. Some examples are Allianz Arena (Allianz is a financial services company), Bet365 Stadium (if someone has missed it,

Bet365 is a betting company), King Power Stadium (King Power Stadium is a travel retail group) and Vodafone Arena (Vodafone is a telecom company).

· The evolution of football shoes

Football shoes, also called cleats or soccer boots, are special footwear that is worn while playing football (soccer). They are specifically designed for the pitch and the cleats on the sole of the shoe aid the grip during the game. Football boots are by no means a new concept, but they have evolved throughout time thanks to technology and better research.

· The Early Days

Before the year 1891, football boots weren't in use. Instead, the players wore work boots. These were obviously hard to maneuver in and quite heavy on the foot. They weren't designed for people to run in or to kick a ball with. Furthermore, they usually had a reinforced toe, sometimes made of steel; this led to injuries whenever one player accidentally kicked another. They also didn't have any kind of additional grip since there was a regulation that footballers couldn't wear any shoes with anything sticking out from them.

A revision around 1891 allowed football shoes to utilize small bars or studs on the shoes. Soon after that, work boots were replaced with actual football boots designed with leather in order to better perform in the sport. They were made of thick leather and were still quite heavy (about 0.5kg dry and heavier if wet). They also laced up the ankle for better protection. This was the beginning of the modern football boots we know of today.

· The 1900s

The early decades of the 1900s saw little change for football shoes. The World Wars and their aftermaths left little materials for new creations and, frankly, with so many men involved in the war efforts, the demand for updated boots wasn't there. During this time, however, Valsport and Gola were the popular brands marketed to footballers.

After World War II developers and players took an interest in the sport and the footwear again. At this time, football boots began to change noticeably. New technology and research allowed developers to create flexible boots that were much lighter on the foot. The idea of protecting the players' feet took a backseat to the primary concern of better agility and performance. Besides being lighter, the new football boots also came up a little lower on the leg to improve flexibility. These lower boots were especially popular in places like Southern Europe and South America where conditions were less muddy than England.

In the 1950s, Adidas introduced their own football boot that came with screw-in studs that were interchangeable. The studs were either rubber or plastic and were specifically made to be used in different weather or field conditions. This meant that football players no longer had to have two different pairs of shoes, they could use one boot with interchangeable studs instead.

Over time, football boots became even lighter, but the real change came in their designs. Throughout the early years and into the mid-1900s the boots only came in black, but around the 1970s designers began to experiment with different colors. The material was going through a time of experiments and improvements as well. During this footwear revolution, the most popular and famous football boot was created. It was known as the Predator by Adidas. With rubber strips of the same material used a tennis bat in the top of the shoes the power and the amount of spin on the ball was increased. It was a worldwide sensation.It was also during this time that professional players were receiving endorsements to wear specific brands of football boots.

In the final years of the 1900s and into the new millennium football shoes evolved further in terms of the soles of the boots. The change came about as developers saw a need for more flexibility. Since there are cleats on the underside of football boots, they were a little stiff to best support the studs. The new developments during this time allowed for the soles to best support the cleats while providing better flexibility and a better range of motion. This evolution was done by most brands but Adidas's Predator still help the top position in terms of use and sales.

· **Present Day Trends**

Thanks to laser technology, football shoes are now able to be customized to best fit an individual's foot. This is a popular trend with professional footballers. Personalization is also a popular option nowadays. For example, professionals now choose to have their name and sometimes their jersey number on their customized boots. The studs were also updated to more of a blade for better grip on the pitch. Rubber and plastic studs are, however, still available. Further technological developments that are believed to continue as the sport grows in popularity are the use of microchips and tracking tools. These are small computerized devices that will be placed in the shoe and allow a player to track their movements and their performance either on a computer or on their smartphone.

- **Different Types of Shoes**

Up until now, all of the football boots that have been discussed have been for outdoor use. In addition, there are indoor football boots that are slightly different than the outdoor variety. The indoor football shoes are built to be used on flat, hard surfaces instead of a grass pitch. These boots have rubber soles with no studding so they have a better grip on hard floors.

It should also be noted that screw-in studs have fallen out of favor due to the frequency of stud-related injuries caused by the metal cleats. Football clubs, like Manchester United, have also issued bans on bladed boots after players were injured.

- **Shoes Brands**

Adidas was the most popular brand for a while, but nowadays there are a number of popular brands. Companies like Nike and Umbro compete right alongside Adidas with big name players endorsing the different brands. Thanks to these endorsements, Nike and Adidas seem to be the most popular brands of football boots with big stars like Cristiano Ronaldo promoting them on and off the pitch. Over the years, football shoes have taken on different sizes, shapes, and colors, but the main goal of developers have always been providing players with the best possible performance. As technology advances, you can be sure that football boots will continue to evolve, too.

Thank You

Thank You For Reading This Book And Shared This Book To Friends As Birthday Gift Have A Wonderfull Day .

www.ingramcontent.com/pod-product-compliance
Lightning Source LLC
Chambersburg PA
CBHW022231170726
47990CB00022B/1199